LES GRANDES
ROUTIÈRES

France's Classic Grand Tourers

LES GRANDES ROUTIÈRES

France's Classic Grand Tourers

William Stobbs

Foulis

Haynes

A **FOULIS** Motoring Book

First Published 1990

© William Stobbs & Haynes Publishing Group 1990

Published by:
Haynes Publishing Group
Sparkford, Nr Yeovil, Somerset
BA22 7JJ

British Library Cataloguing in Publication Data
Stobbs, William
Les grandes routieres.
1. French cars, history
I. Title
629.2220944

ISBN 0-85429-716-2

Principal Photographer: David Sparrow
Editor: Mansur Darlington
Page layout: Mike King
Cover design: Camway Autographics
Printed in England by: J.H. Haynes & Co. Ltd
Typeset in 11/12pt Garamond light roman

CONTENTS

6
FOREWORD
by Philippe Charbonneaux

9
ACKNOWLEDGEMENTS

10
1 CIVILISATION
The fruits of the thirties

12
2 FRANCE
La Gloire versus Chaos

20
3 HOTEL LIFE
The move to the Palace Hotels

28
4 TRAVEL
in the twenties and thirties

36
5 HISPANO-SUIZA
& Marc Birkigt

68
6 BUGATTI
& Ettore

106
7 DELAGE
Louis de l'Age d'Or

138
8 DELAHAYE
& three engineers

152
9 TALBOT-LAGO
& Anthony Lago

172
TECHNICAL SPECIFICATIONS

182
PHOTO CREDITS

FOREWORD

by Philippe Charbonneaux

The principal element of an automobile is its coachwork. Prototypes are always presented by a photograph of the ensemble, machinery coming later.

Around 1938 I used to visit the workshops of the coachbuilders working in the suburbs of Paris, and my curiosity eventually gave me an understanding of the methods of each and all of them.

As a young designer I used to show them my drawings, with the hope of finding a master coachbuilder one day who might do me the honour of using all, or at least a part, of my inspirations and projects. Fortunately, Figoni, master of curves and elegant lines, found my ideas acceptable and complementary to his own. He was very much an artist, often forgetful of immediate work in progress, while dreaming of new ideas.

Henri Chapron would never admit to having accepted so much as a vague suggestion, let alone an idea, from anyone at all. That is why his coachwork was never revolutionary, reflecting only his classical spirit. He was positively allergic to the risks involved in making even the most sensible innovation. Like Figoni, however, he always produced finished work of consummate skill and perfection.

Saoutchik, on the contrary, took every possible risk. Nicknamed 'Violet le Duc', he never hesitated to embellish with chrome or even gilt. Obsessed with form, he cared little for cooling the engine even, and he was never heard to make remarks like Emile Mathis' slogan, 'Weight is the enemy'. Visual magic is what he was after.

Franay was a great coachbuilder of real quality, whose establishment completely lost its reputation when he disappeared. The workshop then contented itself with repair work. Their last work of any consequence was the Citroën 15CV, which I designed entirely, and it should never have had the name Franay. The enterprise was then taken over by Chapron.

Labourdette's origins are well known. John Henry, whom I knew very well, was an outstanding romancer and man of the world, who knew how to satisfy his clients. He achieved renown in particular for the 'skiff' designs which he originated; inspired by boats, the planks joined by copper rivets. Polished and varnished, they gave an appearance of speed, luxury and originality, but his other designs were often banal. He did not like young designers.

Dubosc produced well-finished coachwork and I had the opportunity to design several Delahaye 135Ms, 175s and 180s, as well as a Talbot-Lago 4.5 for him.

Antem had advanced ideas and I often collaborated with them. One of the first to abandon wood framework, their coachwork was light and full of quality, and working with them was always satisfying. I designed the Delahaye 235 and also many public vehicles which were made by them.

I also knew many of the French coachbuilders like Guilloré and Heuliez le Bastard as well as Italians like the great Pinin Farina, Ghia, Touring and Mono.

I was fortunate to live and work in that great period in which coachbuilders, heirs of the horse carriage era, produced such outstanding work. They were all artists, giving their best to everything they produced, with love. What a visual feast it was to see them at their work in all the various skilled areas; tracing, planing, sheet metal forming, painting, leatherwork, and so on. So many *métiers* of art, alas all gone, as well as so many talented artists.

The coachbuilders disappeared with the introduction of mass production, its speed and the necessity to save time, as well as the necessity to follow the same tendencies and repetition. Those who could not face up to these changes were doomed.

The automobile is always changing, new materials like the various plastics taking the place of those of yesterday. Sheet metal has had its day.

The truth is, that which appears impossible today will be tomorrow's money spinner.

ACKNOWLEDGEMENTS

Those listed here provided the knowledge, and their experience, their time and humour, some outstanding meals, and the fabulous cars themselves, which in most cases had taken them at least ten years to resurrect. There are no words adequately to thank them except to say that this is their book, a fact which they will realise when they see their cars. The four names at the end of the list are the photographers, who gave their time and expertise to provide some art as well as details for the cognoscenti. Sotheby's and Christies have also given their knowledge, experience, and photographs for which we are very grateful.

Photo credits and, where known, the cars' owners can be found at the end of the book.

Lady Howe
José Lesur
Patrick Delage
Dominique Dupont
Philippe Looten
Bernard Heurteux
Bernard Parris
Frank Annett
Chris Renwick
Rod Grainger
Mansur Darlington
Ian Finlater
Anders Ditlev Clausager
Geoffrey Ward
The late Hugh Conway
Geoffrey Perfect
Peter Agg
John Wilson
David Heimann
Ivan Dutton
Richard Pilkington
Adrian Liddell
Ray Middleton
John Walker
Brian Dearden-Briggs
Jean-Paul Dubroca
Jules M. Heumann
Paul Atterton
Malcolm Barber

Sotheby's
Christies
Charles Howard
Andrew Morland
Dan Margulies
John Merryfield
Bob Roberts
Philippe Charbonneaux
Claude Viry
Michael Tyler
Karl Sargent
Harry Payne
GRW Wickham
CRW Hampton
Roland Poncet
Guido Bartolomeo
Roger Tanguy
Robert Delaplace
M. Potelle
Alain Ballaret
Tom Bowhill
John Perrit
Harry Payne
Philip Scott
David Sparrow
Jerry McCabe
Len Smith
Max de Roche

CIVILISATION

The fruits of the thirties

Civilisation's best artifacts are becoming a many coloured multi-racial conglomerate, stored in museums and retrieval systems, widely disseminated by the media but, as never before, auctioned. Christies and Sotheby's catalogues can relate the current value of a Bugatti to a Rembrandt, or a Hispano-Suiza to a 3000-year-old Egyptian sculpture. But in all cases, however stupefyingly high the auction price, this is not really the crucial issue. It is the fact that these artifacts are alive with the essence of a time, place and spirit. Recognised now as works of moving art, their value will continue to increase 'considerably'.

Time was, when vintage cars were kept alive by amateur engineers as a compulsive hobby; nothing to do with profit and loss whatsoever; everyone thought we were gone in the head. Why not a round of golf, so much healthier? Gilt-edged securities now, the standards of restoration have reached heights of high-tech 'commensurate' with the prices. Meanwhile the early collectors are no longer cranks, but respected *cognoscenti*. There are fakes about, but also chassis numbers, documented provenance and obscure but essential knowledge collected by specialists in each marque, all of which is vital to collect before you become as dizzy as a whipping top with the bidding. And bid at auctions you must. Buying from dealers puts the collector into an immediate long term loss of five to ten years. The only way a private collector can make sense is by buying at auction in competition with the dealer, and out-bid him at the point when he knows that the dealer's margin of profit has been whittled away, as he surely needs more to retain his establishment than you do.

The special fruits of the thirties, which are now maturing again of course, are the Bugattis. They were just right in the years when first created and being hand-made by Ettore and his craftsmen at Molsheim. Everyone with any feeling about automobiles wanted one. Then they went 'off', for various reasons, and, as Hugh Conway, world authority on Bugatti, wrote in *Grand Prix Bugatti* (G.T. Foulis & Co Ltd, 1968 and 1983), 'A thousand pounds worth of Bugatti in 1929, could be had for 100 in 1940, 400 in 1950 and 4000 in 1968'. As everyone knows, a Bugatti Royale sold for £5½ million in 1988, and the Type 55 two-seater roadsters have been selling at £240,000 and up. The coupés and cabriolets of all the Routières here are nowhere near the values which they deserve and will reach long before 2000. And they are satisfying things to own, more useful than a Louis XIV Secretaire or a Tang horse.

FRANCE

la Gloire versus Chaos

France has retained her grandeur, despite Napoleonic wars, revolution, two world wars and the Common Market, because art is endemic to her. At her peak, Chenonceaux, Blois, Amboise, the Impressionist and post-Impressionist painters - she is quite something. At her least, France has style: a Renaissance lute, whalebone corsets of the 1890s, or a *deux chevaux*. There has always been a continuity of design and craftsmanship, the horse carriages of the 1750s being echoed in the *carrosserie* of the 1930s. But just as the owners of the landaus and barouches were stopped in their tracks by the guillotine, the owners of the Routières of the thirties were pulled up short by the radical changes due to the Second World War.

There is a tendency to dismiss the collapse of the thirties and the disappearance of the Routières as the result of the 1929 Wall Street crash, followed by the results of the American depression moving across the Atlantic, closely followed by the evils of Hitler. It was more complicated than that. There were political mazes and financial hysteria which removed the gold standard and devalued the franc, together with continual technological changes.

A major issue which was to affect everything irrevocably was the changing class system. England in this respect led a sheltered life compared with Europe, where the coronets had been rolling with the heads for some time. Germany, Tzarist Russia and the Austro-Hungarian Empire had been reduced to impotence. The ancient empire of the Hapsburgs had disintegrated into the five states of Austria, Hungary, Yugoslavia, Czechoslovakia and Romania. The Austrian Empire had been liquidated in fact - a short sentence for an enormous fact.

Russia was in a state of administrative collapse, after the failure of the dream of world communism predicted between 1917 and 1920. Russian isolation was presently consecrated in the Stalin slogan 'socialism in one country', but many Europeans were getting the hang of a pink form of it, France not least with its strikes of 1936. The idea of equality was beginning to change Europe by not only removing the *ancien régime*, but by giving power to the workers, who were showing muscle in demanding more pay, better conditions and paid holidays. The improvements to workers' conditions became everywhere apparent, not least in the small economical cars which were appearing for everyman; jaunty and full of verve, they were the precursors of the current world cars.

For a century, France had been financially buoyant. The franc was as solid as a rock in the twenties, until it was saddled with a colossal public debt. Large sums borrowed by the Tsars would never be repaid by the Communists. The Government had also borrowed from the Bank of France and the USA to carry out enormous repairs due to the unimaginable damage of the First World War. Meanwhile, Germany continually evaded her disarmament obligations, as well as reparation payments.

Despite these problems, France still not only had *La Gloire*, but was also the centre of the international money market. The economy of France was one in which all hands were at work in 1926, with only 585 unemployed. With the help of 3 million immigrant workers, industrial productivity had increased by 38 per cent since 1918. Overall prosperity was reflected in higher living standards, reduced working hours and the adoption of Britain's 'le weekend'.

There were also alluring consumer goods, such as bicycles, automatic telephones, the cinema, wireless sets, while Citroën, Renault and Peugeot together produced 2,600,000 cars in 1928. French aviators such as Saint-Exupéry and Mermoz were developing long-distance air services, while Costes and Lebrix flew from Paris to Washington, via Africa and South America. Amy Mollison flew to Australia (and then bought a Delage D8), and Lindbergh flew across the Atlantic in the *Spirit of Saint Louis,* a single-engined plane, in 33 hours 32 minutes. Alcock and Brown had already flown it, with the advantage of Rolls-Royce Eagle engines, in 16 hours 27 minutes in 1919, in the opposite direction.

A new form of snobbery appeared in the twenties. It required that value take precedence over title, talent over wealth, and creative ability over establishment. France was supreme on the continent and remained so for a decade, because it was more aware of this fact than the other Europeans.

The hegemony she exercised in the political world was unquestionably apparent also in the realms of culture. Paris, *La Ville Lumière,* had outstanding figures in all the arts: in literature, Proust, Gide, Valéry, Claudel, Duhamel, Maurois, Malraux and Cocteau; in painting, Picasso, Braque, Gauguin, Matisse, Soutine, Miro, Chagall, Chirico, Dali and Duchamp. And, of course, Isadora Duncan in the dance, and Josephine Baker. The profound disarray of old established ideas of society was becoming increasingly obvious all over Europe, but the new concepts, and the arts which mirrored them, almost all started in Paris.

Despite all this, the franc fell to 243 to the pound sterling in 1927. My grandfather, a draughtsman-engineer, specialising in locomotives, took me to France that year; by train naturally. I can remember not only the French locomotives and the marvellous food, the fabulous landscapes and the bullock-carts, but also my grandfather's euphoria at this new value of the pound. The pre-war rate had been 25 francs to the pound, now it was worth ten times as much to an Englishman abroad. So there was now a furore about the franc from everyone in France.

With typical gallic fervour, everyone said that it was 'essential for France's honour, prestige and credit to restore the old monetary value'. In 1928 Poincaré did stabilise the franc, at 125 to the pound. It has been said that of all the financial decisions made between the wars, this is the only one that was not a blunder. The franc had been preserved; but wait.

The French Communist party was growing. On May Day 1929, gendarmes made more than 4000 arrests in Paris. Meanwhile, as though to underline the changes in society, the leaders of the *ancien régime* were actually dying. Foch was given a State funeral at the Arc de Triomphe; Clemenceau was buried 'without manifestations, invitations or rites'. In government, chaos was winding itself up. In 1928 there were nine different Cabinets. New men were appearing. Arrogant, scintillating and authoritarian, they replaced the honest and upright ones like Aristide Briand, who was ill (he died in 1932). The 'Era of Illusions' was ending, they said in *Le Monde*. But what would replace the illusions? There was a positive answer to this: Black Thursday, 24 October 1929, the American Wall Street Crash.

France thought nothing of it, at first. Industrial production actually increased until 1930. France's relatively backward economic habits cushioned it from the faster moving countries of the USA, Germany and Great Britain. Devaluation had made France a cheap country for tourism and foreign purchasers, which camouflaged the coming catastrophe. The franc was now stable, and French gold reserves were rising even. In 1920, Britain had 2 million unemployed, Germany 3 million, and France only quarter of a million, but the end was coming, none the less, and quickly. The earthquake

started when France refused to help the Austrian Kredit Anstalt Bank, which caused a run on German reserves, and also the pound in London. The real bomb under the status quo was put in place by President Hoover, who prescribed a year's moratorium on international payments. London, now the centre of the international banking system, had not sufficient gold, went off the gold standard and devalued the pound. Twelve other countries followed suit and the international monetary system collapsed. Germany was in the worst state of inflation. It is rumoured that Mercedes rode through that period by printing money on a press in the Archives Department. The United States then demanded an instalment of her war debt from France. France refused, of course, and the French Cabinet fell. From December 1932 to December 1933, four successive governments wrestled and then collapsed. There were bankruptcies galore. Roosevelt's devaluation of the dollar, in March 1933, was another blow to France, still, strangely, on the gold standard. It meant that France's export prices had now increased by 30 per cent. Production declined further, and unemployment soared to a million.

There was corruption as well. Stavisky, an elegant swindler, was arrested, together with his collaborator, for floating bonds for millions of francs. The partner-in-crime was a previous president, named Paul Boncoor. A judge who organised their release was the brother-in-law of the then Prime Minister, Chautemps. Then Stavisky was found murdered, and 'Action Française' denounced Chautemps, who resigned. He was succeeded by Daladier, but there were demonstrations of a strong anti-government nature, five hours of fighting and a thousand people injured. Parliament had been completely discredited. 'It appeared that France was failing to adjust her social and political system to meet the demands of the modern world,' said the New York *Herald Tribune*, in a cool tone, disregarding the fact that it was Hoover and Roosevelt who had set off this débâcle.

In 1933, after the fall of the French Government, Hitler became the German Chancellor, with his inimitable smile, which hinted at something unthinkable to come. By the Spring of 1936, France was in dire straits. Poverty gripped the working class as well as the bourgeoisie. Bankruptcies doubled and unemployment trebled. At the election, the Popular Front won - a resounding defeat for the right. For the first time in French history, the head of the government was a socialist and a Jew, Léon Blum. A wave of strikes rolled across France and women joined the movement this time, en masse, taking over the premises of many establishments including 'Galeries Lafayette' and 'Printemps'. The women also wanted the vote, of course, but did not receive it until 1944. Nineteen thirty-six is the time when Bugatti was not allowed to enter his own factory at Molsheim, and Chanel was barred entry to her *maison de couturier,* among hundreds of similar examples.

Simultaneous with the strikes of 1936 which amounted to a minor revolution, there were fabulous balls and parties in Paris, reported in the *New Yorker* by the French correspondent Janet Flauner, 'From May, through July, from 1935 to 1939, Paris saw an endless stream of masked balls in the magnificently furnished apartments of the beau monde'. But this was France. *La Gloire* even presided over the strikers (not merely the rich) who organised their socialist demonstrations in Paris at the 'Maison de la Culture', with banners and posters saluting Daumier, Zola, Molière, Racine, Voltaire, Seurat, Manet and Rodin at the same time as they put forward their demands for the right of workers to rest for a week in the summer.

Instantly, panic struck Deauville and Biarritz, Cannes and Nice, where the sunbathing upper classes had enjoyed a privacy which was now to be destroyed. In 1939 they were to have the Germans as well. This period was the stomping ground for Figoni et Falaschi, Saoutchik, Chanel, Letourneur et Marchand, Fernandez & Darrin and Bugatti. It is incredible that such beauty and originality could blossom out of that knife-edge of catastrophe and chaos.

HISPANO-SUIZA K6, 1936, Fernandez & Darrin.

18

3

HOTEL LIFE

The move to the Palace Hotels

Everyday life to match that of the chateaux of the Loire was no longer possible in the twenties and thirties, nor desirable either, so French society conjured up a new way of life - the Palace Hotel - which began to proliferate in Europe in the early thirties, in the same way that the enormous demands for seaside holidays of the current working class has spawned the multi-storey hotels which have so radically changed seaside landscapes all over Europe and America. But these anonymous concrete apartments, plus small hire cars and air travel, are a new problem. Let us return to the Grandes Routières, who got to their hotels by road, with plenty of luggage.

They say that the first move to hotels from palaces was taken by Napoleon III and the Empress Eugènie, who had the Villa Eugénie built at Biarritz, from which they attended to all the affairs of State, simultaneously with firework displays, tableaux vivants and with Grand Balls for the few Royals still left. The Villa Eugénie was renamed the Palais de Biarritz, but when it was joined rather closely by the Casino, it was renamed Hotel du Palais. The Duke of Albe had set up the Casino and made it quite irresistible, partly because of his *outré* interior decorations, but mainly because of his wild life-style, which pervaded the place and was as infectious as his roulette wheels. Living it up in style had started in a grand way with *la belle époque*, of fifteen years before the First World War and ten years after it, but actually it kept on and on, after the 'naughty nineties' which had set the high note like a weird tuning fork, to *Le Moulin Rouge, Les Folies Bergères* and the Can-Can, then on to the Charleston, negro jazz and Josephine Baker.

The stage had actually been set architecturally for all the Grand Hotels of Europe by the Paris Opera House, designed by Charles Garnier, which had an architectural idiom easy to imitate.

The Opera itself provided an elaborate social ritual, with a setting in which the spectators were also actors, those of high rank or outstanding *succès de scandale* in the boxes, where they were quite as much on show as the singers on the stage. Opera glasses were designed for watching those in the boxes - who wants to see the larynx of a tenor on peak frenzy? It is the same today, in Paris, Milan, New York and Covent Garden; those caged in the boxes being watched as keenly as Great Crested Grebes by ornithologists.

History was sometimes transferred from the

Royal Palaces to the Grand Hotels. The Emperor of Austria, for example, died at 'Beau Rivage' at Geneva. The cortège started from the hotel, black plumed horses and all. Some monarchs spent their entire lives in them, leaving ghosts which have subsequently been replaced by the phantoms of racketeers, heavy industry or armament magnates, disgraced politicians, or the Princes of tiny Principalities, but, above all, by real live widows of all the above, varying in shape from near wraiths to enormous creatures; but each and every one perched securely in her own estimate of her place in society.

César Ritz organised a great number of these hotels throughout the West: in Paris, Rome, Madrid, New York, Budapest, Montreal, Philadelphia and Pittsburg, which made his name famous as the showman who set the stages for star performances by his clientele, such as the King of the Belgians and the King of Wurtemberg.

Many Royals had had by now one waltz too many, and had also moved out into hotel life, the facts of their existence being collected by historians into serious archives, while politics, fêtes, history and the beau monde were all taking place in the huge hotels, which were crazily expensive to live in, but nowhere near so much as keeping a staff of 40 to 100 servants in each household.

Staying in one grand hotel could be boring, so they moved regularly, at first by horse carriages, followed by Pullman trains, and in the twenties and thirties by the Grandes Routières which were created for this purpose.

Grand Hotels as a category constitute a microcosm, set apart from the world. It was possible to live continuously in them, the concièrge and head waiter knowing likes and dislikes in all things.

Each Ritz had a Palm Court, because wise old women had advised César that such an atmosphere is congenial for romance. Doors for a good 'entrance' were organised. Mirrors were everywhere, for women to check make-up, deportment and to watch unobtrusively other women at their work. Without these players, the Ritz hotels would have been costly failures, and it is remarkable what feasts of anecdotal associations they have provided for novelists, with balls, cuisine, couture, oysters, champagne and the nostalgia of a past world, well laced with sin. The Countess of Warwick, for example, engineering her blackmail of Edward VII from the Paris Ritz, King Zog of Albania arriving

with his luggage trunks so full of gold in 1940 that no one could carry them, the Aga Khan keeping a permanent suite there for forty years, and all the while Oliver Dabescat seemed to be *maître d'hôtel*, so that Marcel Proust wrote about him when young, and Harold Nicholson when he was as old as a tortoise, saying that he was everlastingly 'blending with masterly precision, the servile, the protective, the deferential and the condescending', depending on whom he was addressing. Distinguishing uppercrust from yuppies is too easy. What Dabescat was searching for were potentially dangerous snakes with all the right accents and habits, but also an in-built treachery which might give the hotel a bad name; ultimately Real Scandals.

Cosmopolitan society moved ceaselessly, drifting from Paris to Cannes, Monte Carlo to Vienna, Marienbad to Biarritz and then back again, with its retinue of the ancient but rich, the talented, the glamorous, the *grandes-horizontales*, from the *demi-monde*, and star performers of ballet, music and opera. A rich mix. Some travelled by Pullman train, but most in Delage or Hispano-Suiza. This is why the Grandes Routières were made, and how they got their name. Their engines were designed to pull a chassis with luxurious coachwork and a family of four or five, plus some essential luggage. The rest went by train. Arrived at Deauville, they would soon be off to Milan or Biarritz, chauffeur driven. It is a tragedy that not one of the hundreds of chauffeurs of that period ever wrote a memoir about it all. I have been searching the book stalls on the Left Bank for years for such a book, without success. You try.

The Grand Hotels of the thirties had a rating and an incandescent ambience which would go right off the scale of our current standards in the *Guide Michelin*. Take the George V for example, off the Champs Elysées, on the Avenue George V. This was the favourite of Louis Delage, his showroom being close by. This hotel had a special kind of perfection, created by one man - François Dupré - who turned it into a fabulous hotel-museum, with fireplaces, panelling and doors mainly from a Louis XIII chateau which was dismantled near Orleáns. Hollywood stars traditionally stayed there, and so did Mata Hari, who was finally arrested there. After the First World War, it was the French home of the Vanderbilts, the Rockefellers, the Queen of Denmark and, particularly, *haute couture* models, flashing their eyes and teeth in the grill room, where

work-of-art cuisine was often completely ignored by the personalities, scintillating non-stop.

The Bristol also ranks high, the Shah of Persia, in his prime, staying only at the Bristol when in Paris. Close to the best shops in Paris, and also the Elysée Palace, where the President and the ambassadors live. The owner and *maître d'hôtel*, Hippolyte Jammet, was as rich as his clients, with a Fernandez-bodied Hispano-Suiza. He spent twelve million francs on improvements and extensions to his hotel in 1930, and sent his son Pierre to work in the Ritz in Madrid and then the Atlantic in Hamburg, in preparation for taking over the Bristol. When the Second World War started - and this book more or less finishes - German Generals hurried to the Bristol, but the Stars and Stripes flag was at the flagstaff, as old Hippolyte had persuaded the American Ambassador and his staff to move in. They moved out only when the USA joined the Allies - some time later.

The Bristol has many reminders of the genuine old regime: a portrait of Marie Antoinette by Drouhais, a bust of Louis XVI by Pavou, a Gobelin tapestry once owned by Napoleon, and a fine collection of antique furniture.

The Imperial, Vienna, encapsulates some of the real Austro-Hungarian grandeur which had mainly disappeared at the end of the First World War. It has an inimitable ring to it, in place of the pastiche cooked up by many of the so-called Palace Hotels. The Imperial took over the town house of the Duke of Würtemburg and the Emperor Franz-Josef himself declared that it should be named 'Imperial'. Wagner stayed there, while polishing up the final scores of *Tannhäuser* and *Lohengrin*. Hitler stayed there in 1938, sleeping, curiously, in a small back room while Goering had the state suite. His psyche on the wane? The Russians took it over at the end of the Second World War when it was in a very bad state. Between the wars, it had fed and watered the Kings of Belgium, Denmark, Norway, Nepal, Saudi Arabia and Great Britain, as well as the Queens of Holland and England. There were others such as Gromyko, Kissinger, Sadat, Pompidou, Khrushchev; they are invariably a curious assortment, those in political high places. There are also times when the no doubt efficient directors of companies manufacturing plastics and bathroom fittings, dog foods and tinned fish, or armaments, take over the state apartments together with the Imperial bedroom, to the silent amusement of the hotel cat.

The Paris Ritz also started from the real thing, in the town house of the Duc de Lauzin, at 15 Place Vendôme, in 1896. César Ritz, as everyone knows, was a shepherd's son from Niederwald, a scarcely credible beginning for someone who was to become the Diaghilev of the whole ballet-like hotel-society life, world-wide. Ritz did not reach this world acclaim with flair alone, he worked at it. He was at the Imperial, Vienna, at the Grand, Monte Carlo, the Minerva, Baden, and the Savoy, London, where he worked with Escoffier who was so often burning himself on the charcoal stove, being so short, before they both set up at the Paris Ritz. Then they took over the Society of Europe, lock, stock and barrel. The garage of the Ritz was another world, which I knew very well, like a global showroom of Grandes Routières: Cadillacs, Packards, Duesenbergs, Rolls-Royce Phantoms I & II, Bentley $6\frac{1}{2}$s & 8s, and, of course, all the French routières in this book.

The Paris Ritz in itself was actually a microcosm of the very strange thirties world peopled by personalities who were chauffeured about in Hispanos and Delages, like King Ferdinand of Romania, King Alfonso of Spain, the Maharajah of Kapusthala, Barbara Hutton and the Aga Khan. Then there were the others, the owner-drivers, who drove Bugattis and Delahayes or Talbot-Lagos, like Ernest Hemingway, Malcolm Campbell and Coco Chanel.

There are three bars at the Paris Ritz, but the real one was just inside the Rue Cambon entrance. During the thirties they drank fearful cocktails like Pink Lady, Gin & Sin, Chatterley, Monkey Gland, Bees Knees, C.P. (Cole Porter); and Rainbow, which was anisette, mint, yellow chartreuse, cherry brandy, kummel, green chartreuse and cognac in equal portions, shaken. This tight-rope so many people were walking, over the disarray of established values and the rejection of so many obsolescent ideas, needed a pick-me-up from time to time. The heat of this melting pot was becoming uncomfortable by 1939.

The world of the great hotels is a different way of life from any other. A world of unshakeable assumptions about the proper way of doing everything, for example. Before the Second World War, the staff silently watched aristocrats and the rich in business from morning till night. Their standards were high, whatever the clients'. They knew how to perform their duties and were tipped

considerably more than they are today. It was all at a different, less opportunist level. Both clients and staff have changed radically and it needs a different book to describe quite how. The cars have changed as well, of course.

4

TRAVEL

in the twenties and thirties

Travel by car seemed perfectly natural at the time. Nothing unusual. Continuously high speeds were impossible because neither the roads nor the engines would stand for it. The very distant past of carriages with matched teams of horses and the Grand Tour were no doubt fabulous - for the coachman - but suffocatingly slow by our standards. The Veterans and Edwardians had real style, but so many punctures you wouldn't believe.

Basically, thirties travel had to do with pace. Leisured sufficiently to retain some elegance even, it was based on the assumption that the driver and his friends had no other concern or demands on their time than the enjoyment of the journey.

Present motorways are civilized, even impeccable at their best, and indispensable. There is little to see, though, except streams of cars and lorries. The food at the service stations is getting better, but is basic to say the least. Also there is an atmosphere approaching panic to get either here or there, and it is this which deteriorates the psyche. Other people did not impinge so much in the days of the Routières. The calm, the noise of the engine, the changing landscape and the conversation, all of which have gone, replaced with cassettes instead of ideas, a whirligig of traffic instead of landscape, and other cars too near and too fast, especially the high-wheeled lorries in the rain. Then, in the thirties, we arrived relaxed and content, now we get there much sooner but a bit panic-stricken, an accident or a five mile tail-back having upset the timetable.

The roads had a lot to do with it, in France especially, before the motorways. French roads have been outstanding for donkeys' years; as evidence Bentley, Alvis, Aston Martin and Rolls-Royce used them for testing prototypes. These roads did not become the first in Europe without effort. Caesar's roads gave them a head start, but the Goths, more keen on pillage and rape, erased them more or less.

The French road system really started in the 16th century when Henry IV conceived a way to obtain them. He dreamed up the title 'Grand Voyer' which meant 'Road Creator in Excelsis'. It carried real clout and Royal backing. For centuries, a succession of these road men, with varying titles - Bridge and Pavement chief, *Chef de Ponts et Chaussées* - improved the ease of getting across France. The two most outstanding were Daniel Trudaine and his son Philibert, who between them produced 24,800 miles of good roads. Then Pierre Tresagoet in 1815 produced a new kind of road construction a bit like John McAdam's in England.

Carriages and stage coaches benefited, taking only six instead of eighteen days from Paris to Lyon, and twelve days to Toulouse instead of a month. Hoteliers were livid, saying they were ruined, like hotels today by-passed into oblivion by auto-routes.

It was on these splendid white roads, dishevelled by the First World War, that Louis Delage set off on a tour de force in 1920, which improved his sales considerably. He had already created a stir in 1919, by driving from Paris to Nice (905 km) in sixteen hours, a journey normally of three days at that time. He was driving a Delage CO, a six-cylinder tourer, accompanied by William F. Bradley, the most prestigious motoring journalist then in Europe. The 1920 tour was right round France, 5000 km, which he completed in six days, again with William Bradley. Louis had just opened his showroom at 140 Champs Elysées and needed to put Delage into a limelight occupied by right of quality by Hispano-Suiza and Bugatti, and hogged by Panhard-Levassors and Renaults, which the elderly upper crust continued to buy due to habit, like the British Royals kept buying Daimlers when Rolls-Royce were better in every way.

Road travel in the twenties and thirties included limousines in which one could sleep while the chauffeur steered the car through the night. I have done this many times, as I enjoy driving through the night, but have invariably found the sleeping travellers to be surly and downright ungrateful in the morning. 'We are now in Zurich,' I say with quiet satisfaction, 'Last night you were in Paris.' 'I need a drink, a shave, shower, croissant and coffee and maybe a massage, all my bones and muscles are stuck together. I wish we were still in Paris.' A Rolls-Royce Phantom II was so equipped for Lord Louis Mountbatten. Delage produced his Type GL in 1925, which was adapted for this, and there were high hopes at Delage that it would sound the death knell for Hispano. This was not to be. Planchon, the engineer for this project, had been given everything he asked to make it the perfect Delage, but actually it turned out to be too fragile. Louis Delage fired Planchon. There are now very few GLs about, so no doubt Louis was right.

Four years later Delage produced a really outstanding Grande Routière in the D8; it was driven by Louis regularly from Paris to Nice in his notorious social life, women finding him irresistible apparently. All engineers are *ipso facto* knowledgeable

HISPANO-SUIZA H6B, 1931, Duquesne.

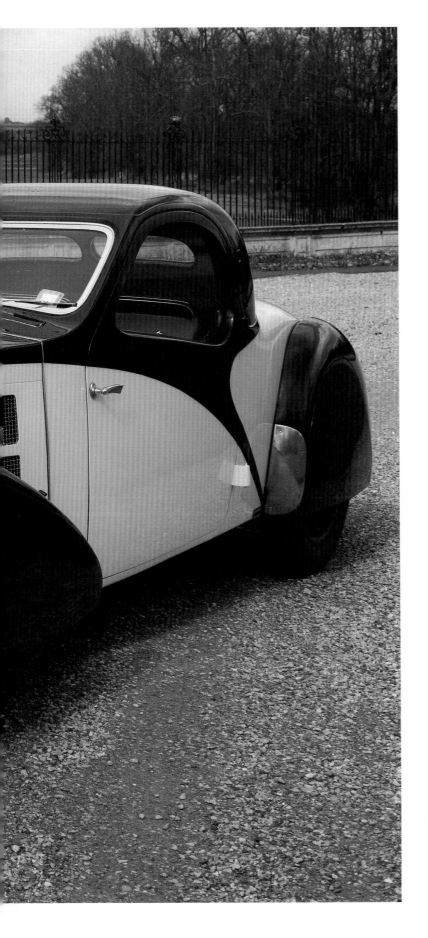

drivers: Louis Delage gave it more of a sense of theatre. Marc Birkigt was also a driver; the perfection of the Hispano was due partly to the fact that he tested them himself including long journeys from France to Spain and back.

Whereas long distance travel today is usually by air, in the twenties it was by rail or liner, with steam engines producing the power in both cases. After a slow start compared with the UK, France having only 2,500 miles of railway track in 1890, compared with Germany's 3,726, England's 6,521, and America's 9,283 miles, France nevertheless was first in putting on the grandeur. Napoleon had the first Royal train, with separate dining, sleeping and observation cars; the prototype, in fact, of all subsequent grand trains from Pullman to the Blue Train.

Keen on speed, the French adopted Thomas Crampton's engines in 1849 and followed this up with a system of coupled driving wheels, their own invention, with startling results. Meanwhile Wilhelm Schmidt's superheated steam pushed the output to a previously unimaginable 1500 bhp for the best locomotives. When I was ten years old, my engineer-draughtsman grandfather, whom you met in Chapter 1, took me with him to France when visiting his French steam-engine colleagues. Even just standing beside locomotives with driving wheels seven feet high, polished steel linkages and steam everywhere, was mind-blowing. Rides on the foot plate have no contemporary equivalent. The wind, noise, flames, steam, vibration and speed, the driver as still as a figurehead, Grandfather with his hat pulled down to his eyes, watch in hand, stoker sweating and stoking madly.

It was not surprising that Woolf Barnato in his Bentley $6\frac{1}{2}$ should race the Blue Train and beat it, the new speed machine, the car, racing the old superhuman steam locomotive with its divine-right-of-way on its own track. No one seems interested in racing the TGV - yet.

By the time I was fourteen, Grandfather had left the LNER and was concerned with cars, during which period we once drove to the south of France in a Minerva, he telling me about Knight sleeve-valves while I watched the Hispanos going by like something out of this world. There were also carts being pulled by oxen in France at that time; so you have missed quite a lot, reader, unless you are of a certain age.

Today's travellers have accepted with tame

acquiescence the low weight-limits imposed on luggage for air passengers, which has almost killed stone-dead the ancient art of 'baggage'.

Designers of limousines and sedancas in the twenties and thirties were also preoccupied in keeping the overall weight down, but not so much.

Gucci, Hermes, Loewes and Louis Vuiton, the high-quality leathersmiths, all without exception started way back in the carriage era. Louis Vuiton began in 1834 in Paris, at Rue Neuve des Capucines. He used to supervise all the packing for the Empress Eugénie, a decent start, when she and her ladies-in-waiting were off to Biarritz for the summer season. The big Renaults took them there, with those rails on the roof to keep the hat boxes from falling off; boxes full of art millinery including flowers, fruit and birds for females to carry on their heads, while their torsos were improved by whalebone corsets, a different kettle of fish from the girls of the eighties who, de rigueur, must coil like a snake into the back seat of a Porsche or XR3, unless she is the lucky one in the front seat.

Vuiton started with domed, hairy leather trunks for the backs of carriages, but changed faster than the others to light-weight stackable trunks on wooden frames, right for liners or limousines.

It was customary for Letourneur et Marchand, Chapron and Saoutchik to show their latest bodywork designs to the luggage makers to have trunks made to measure and the luckiest of the vintage cars still have them in the boot. Many chose Vuiton, *père et fils*, because of their perfectionism. Vuiton frames were made of 30-year-old poplar wood, seasoned for four years. This was covered with thin ply panels, canvas covered and bound in leather, and fitted with special five-number locks, each customer having his own number. All metal parts were brass. The fabric has always had the initials LV worked into it, which made it difficult to copy in the past, but now counterfeit Vuiton luggage is made in Italy, Morocco, Thailand and Korea to the tune of several million pounds. World-wide counterfeit is now a fact of life. Some luxury firms grimly smile: the real time to worry, they say, is when their goods are no longer fashionable enough to imitate.

Vuiton luggage was right for the cars of the twenties and thirties, carrying the coachbuilt ambience right into the boot, but don't imagine that such luxury disappeared with the Second World War. The current Vuiton turnover is about 2 billion french francs and the Vuiton Museum, at 78 Avenue Morceau, Paris, shows examples right back to 1890. The director of the museum said quietly that the thirties coachbuilders could have been a little more considerate and less whimsical ('lubie') with the shapes they saddled Vuiton with. It required some ingenuity and extra straps just to get them OUT of deep boots with lids at the top, like the Chapron D8 Delage - its one fault. Some had no access to the boot at all except by removing the back seats - a chauffeur's job then and exasperating for owner-driver now.

The cars of the thirties and those of the eighties show two distinct and different worlds. The thirties world had fewer cars. The eighties world is getting worried, and thinking about more lanes to the motorways and helicopters.

5

HISPANO-SUIZA
& Marc Birkigt

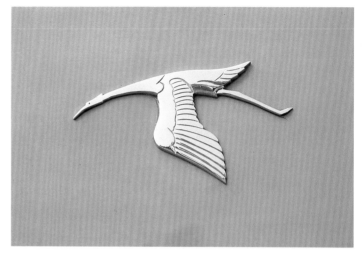

Archive material for both Birkigt and Hispano-Suiza is scarce, because the Civil War destroyed the Spanish factories, and the British destroyed Bois-Colombes in the Second World War. Marc Birkigt, there being few personal stories or documents, is therefore described as a 'shadowy figure'. This is not so. The originality and integrity of every engine he designed gives a clear picture of this man, who could work on problems in silence for hours, and then design both the engine and the machine tools with which to make it, more or less simultaneously. I doubt if there were many stories to tell. Married, he had a son Louis, who worked on aircraft design, and a daughter Yvonne, married to Maurice Heurteux, who worked, post-war, at Bois-Colombes. Birkigt had a villa at Versoix on Lake Geneva, initially for the family, but at the end for himself as well. For relaxation he enjoyed sailing a 12-metre sloop. He also liked walking and Wagner, but above all driving Hispano-Suizas.

Birkigt's life was an obsessional pursuit of perfection in automobile and aero-engine design. He spent many hours at his drawing board, usually at Bois-Colombes. The prototypes were often made at Barcelona, because the machine tools there were particularly good, as well as the specialist founders. Birkigt would drive there and supervise production, to exacting standards, being a perfectionist like Royce and Leland. The prototype completed, he was off testing it by driving to Madrid, and simultaneously to sort out the problems there concerning trucks, at Guadalajara. Then back to Bois-Colombes, with mechanics on board to make adjustments. The prototype would be tested over thousands of Spanish

and French miles, and by Birkigt, sometimes assisted by Zucarelli. Bernard Heurteux, now President of the Hispano-Suiza Club and owner of Birkigt's last, personal, J12, has had several things to say about him. That he got his ideas while driving, for example. I have driven many times between Paris, Barcelona and Madrid between 1930 and 1980 on business, along the roads which Marc Birkigt frequented. In the thirties the French roads were wide, white and splendid with fast moving traffic. The Spanish roads were high-cambered, with carts, pot-holes and ancient trucks, miles of no one at all, and stopping places with wells, with water for people, horses and radiators, always surrounded by children, and with yellow dust everywhere, cars, carburettors and drivers getting covered with its gritty powder.

The traditional inns (still there) with cool courtyards, had quiet, shuttered rooms, with basins and water jugs for travellers, together with a drink of cool sangria. It is easy enough to visualise Marc Birkigt in one of these quiet rooms, thinking about his car, and how it had performed all day on road-test, and making drawings of modifications to improve it. When did he think out that subtle but vital improvement in the leaf springs by changing the fulcrum, making it different for front and rear, and offset . . .? At which parador did he make the drawing changing the transmission, with more ball bearings? Spain was a different world then, living in the past. Tourists were all in the south and on the coast. Around Barcelona and Madrid the tourists were few, and there for the bull rings, or city entertainments, leaving the landscape moonlike in its isolation, fabulous for driving and testing cars like the H6, J12 and K6; a kind of heaven. But he was also designing simpler, more rugged cars for Spain and the Spaniards.

Birkigt's statutory period of military service was fortunately spent entirely in the Ordnance Corps, which equipped him with a knowledge of metallurgy, machine tools and ballistics, an ideal basis, and crucial for what he had to do.

HISPANO-SUIZA H6B

Letourneur

Birkigt's initial lack of success is very encouraging to others who may feel that luck is not always with them, at the start. In 1899, together with two engineers, Velino and Bouvier, he designed an unsuccessful electric bus, which contained an original idea: the batteries were constantly kept full of charge by a generator, driven by a small internal combustion engine. The next year, he designed a car for Emilio Le Cuadra, but two years later, Cuadra was bankrupt, and taken over by J. Castro. He now designed an almost *'pur-sang'* Birkigt, a rough but dependable 2.2-litre four-cylinder T-head with shaft drive, like the future Alfonso seen dimly; but Castro went bankrupt.

Damien Mateu, who took over, was a man of substance with influential friends. It was now 1904, Birkigt was 26, and Fabrica De Automoviles, La Hispano-Suiza, had begun modestly, quietly, in Barcelona: eventually there were showrooms in Madrid, Paris, London and New York. From the beginning, Birkigt received a royalty on every vehicle sold.

Birkigt then spent six hectic and creative years, 1904 - 1910, which eventually resulted in the Alfonso, probably the world's first sports car; fast, spartan and a trend-setter, but he certainly had to bend to it, with the usual mixture of luck and hard work. Married in 1905, Birkigt met King Alfonso

XIII at the 1907 Madrid Show, when he bought three of his 2.2-litre T-heads. The King also mentioned that he was organising the Catalan Cup and needed a Spanish car to win it. Birkigt worked hard, with Louis Pilleverdier and Paolo Zucarelli who had recently joined him. They entered three Hispanos, but could only manage fourth place. The same year, at the Coupe des Voiturettes, it was worse: 5th, 6th and 7th. They increased the capacity

HISPANO-SUIZA H6B

Kellner

to 2.6 litres, raised the compression ratio slightly, and added Rudge wheels for the 1910 Coupe de l'Auto, at Boulogne. Zucarelli was first, Chassagne third and Pilleverdier sixth. Success, which they made sure of by increasing the capacity further, to 3620 cc. The Type 15T Alfonso had arrived, with a claimed 77 mph, but soon they were revolving at Brooklands and elsewhere at 81.5 mph, and everyone wanted one, as they made other sports cars look ugly, and inefficient. The next year Alfonso's Queen, Victoria Eugénie, gave him a white Alfonso for his birthday, with gold-plated fittings and gold wire wheels, very similar to the car in the National Motor Museum at Beaulieu, England. Alfonso immediately drove it from San Sebastian to Madrid at an average of 50 mph. Most people would have gone on making Alfonsos till the cows came home, or developing it into something larger. Birkigt thought otherwise. The Alfonso was the end product of a particular design, and he was right. Side valves were old hat and had nothing to do with an overhead valve future he had already envisaged, with more power, speed, and a lot more torque.

There followed three miserable years, 1910 - 1913. Birkigt designed and made successful trucks at Barcelona, and also devised a system of being paid, in part, by shares in the companies which bought them. A strike at the Barcelona plant then precipitated the move to France, envisaged by sales of the Hispano at the Paris Show. Pilleverdier reconnoitred, and found a bus depot in the Rue Cavé in Levallois-Perret, and the removal of machine tools commenced, together with better lathes, foundry tools and drilling machines. Birkigt believed implicitly in the latest and best technology, metallurgy and machine tools. So of course did all the others: Delage, Bugatti and Lago. A bright light began shining again in 1913. In competition, the 'Sardine', thin with a long tail and a new ohv motor,

set up a record of 150 km/h at Brooklands, and a record at Gaillon, but more important than this, Amos Salvador, Secretary of Defence for Spain, organised a Government subsidy for powerful aero-engines. It makes one pine for the lost archives and the truth, but hearsay has it that Birkigt designed his legendary aero-engine, his first, instantly successful, water-cooled V8, in two months. This is because he had worked it out already, with a car engine.

Eduardo Barton designed the airframe for it, and discussed the type of brake horsepower and torque needed for the power to fly. He was head of the Military Flying School of Cuatro Vientes Aerodrome, and his advice was invaluable.

Birkigt's '12Y' aero-engine weighed only 330 lb by use of alloys, and initially delivered 150 bhp at 1,530 rpm. This was steadily increased to 180, 220 and 320 during the war. It was beautifully simple. The cylinder blocks were two aluminium castings at 90 degrees, crowned by heads with enclosed overhead valve gear, lubricated with oil pumped from and returned to the crankcase. The camshaft drive consisted of shafts and bevel gears driven from the rear end of the crank. The cams acted directly on the valves through mushroom-headed cam followers screwed into the valve stems, with hardened discs between, for adjustment. The H6 car after the war had precisely the same valve design and there are still 129 of them about. Portable gilt-edged securities.

Captain Martinot-Lagarde, of the Service Fabrication d'Aviation Française, saw the V8 aero-engine in Spain on test and had it transported to Chalais-Meudon, where it passed a 50-hour test run.

HISPANO-SUIZA J12

Kellner

A total of 50,000 of these Hispano aero-engines were made during the First World War at factories in France, England and, eventually, the USA. Hispano-Suiza then moved to Bois-Colombes in 1914, with a concentration on the aero-engine, which was also made at six other factories, with a total of 17,000 workers. They were used in various aircraft, but most dramatically in fighters, the British SE5 and the French SPAD. The *'cigogne volante'* was the emblem used in the aircraft of George Guynemer's SPAD *escadrille*. Birkigt had it copied in metal by the

sculptor Bazin, and it was used as the Hispano radiator mascot.

The SPAD French fighter was designed by Louis Bechereau in 1915, and continually developed to the end of the war, but always using the Hispano-Suiza 12Y engine with steadily increasing brake horse power. The SPAD XIII of 1917 was the best, and sadly Guynemer met his death while piloting his. Almost nine thousand SPAD XIIIs were built and supplied to Italy, Russia, Belgium and the USA, so Birkigt's engine was going around the world for anyone to see and appreciate. This was especially so in America, where both Curtiss and Wright modified the connection rods and developed it post-war for US army pursuit-aircraft, raising the power to 320 bhp and calling it the Wright-Hispano.

The Hispano aero-engine was used in several aircraft in Britain, including the AD Flying Boat and, of course, in the SE fighters. There was some trouble with the reduction gears, usually because the gears were sometimes badly made. Often these were removed, and direct drive used instead. At the end of the war, 2,700 SE5s remained, which were mainly sold off to Australia, Poland, Canada and the USA. Some were used in the twenties for 'writing in the sky', the precursor of modern advertising.

HISPANO-SUIZA H6B

Kellner

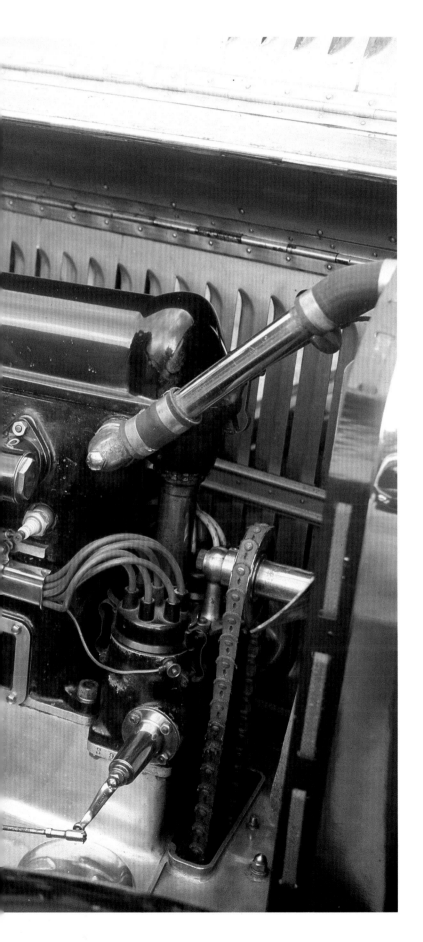

There was considerable interest during the war in the engines and aircraft of the enemy, on both sides. Whenever possible, they were examined minutely by engineers, as more power and manoeuvrability was a matter of life, death and winning. Germany had a head start, of course, because Kaiser Wilhelm had offered a prize for the best engine before the war, in 1913, with technically apt conditions obviously written in by Wilhelm Maybach, designer for Count Zeppelin, and also Paul Daimler. The best German engine was the straight-six Mercedes DIII to DVII and they made a V8 in 1917, but it is arguable that they ever managed more brake horse power and dependability than the Hispano. The Fokker, designed by Reinhold Platz and modified by Rittmeister Von Richthofen, was the best German fighter using the Mercedes engine. Article IV of the Armistice Agreement paid it a particular tribute by singling it out as an item to be handed over to the Allies.

Anthony Fokker had not anticipated this, as he had hoped to start a sensible peace-time business in air travel. Consequently he organised a highly successful smuggling enterprise of 120 aircraft and 400 engines from Germany into Holland, where they were used by the Dutch Army, and as trainers to the Belgian Air Force, and by the Swiss *Fliegertruppe* until 1926.

Meanwhile, from 1914 to 1918, in neutral Spain, the Hispano cars at Barcelona and the Hispano trucks at Guadalajara, continued to be made, with no modifications whatsoever, except the addition of electric lighting which had commenced in the French factory in 1913. It is indicative of the Hispano legend, that when the Master, MB, was otherwise engaged as he indeed was (keeping his aero-engine ahead of the Mercedes, no easy task), everything else should grind on with no alterations.

1934

HISPANO-SUIZA K6

Fernandez & Darrin

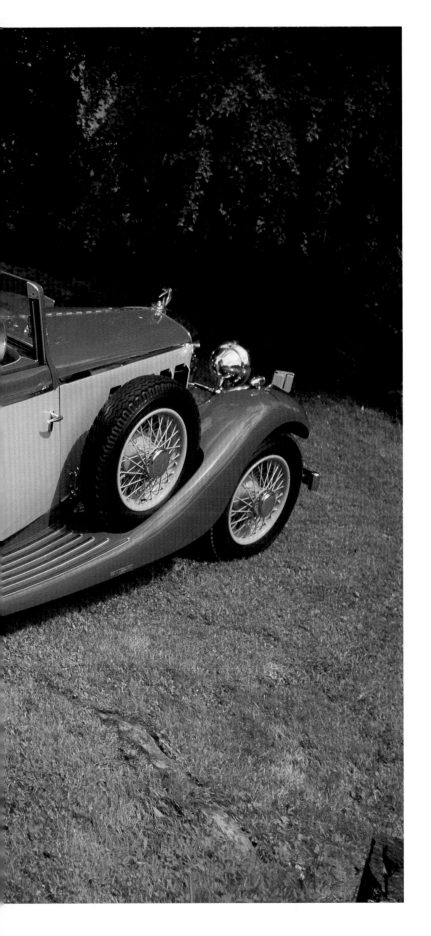

War over, the Spanish Aero Club gave Marc Birkigt a banquet at which he made his simple self-denigratory speech 'I am only an engine designer'. France elected him and Lacoste, his Manager, to the Légion d'Honneur. I know a French vet who got the same for attending brilliantly to some wounded cavalry horses. Surely they could have thought up

HISPANO-SUIZA K6

Binder

something more commensurate with the enormity of the occasion? Aero-engines better than Daimler-Benz?

In 1919 he unveiled the H6 at the Paris Salon, based comprehensively on the V8. The aero-engine had come to earth, 210 lb heavier. It had the same screwed-in steel liners, shaft driven overhead camshafts but coil ignition instead of magnetos and, of course, the four-wheel brakes with gearbox-driven servo. Production output of this car from 1919 to 1931 was 2,661. The effects on all European countries was remarkable, but particularly on France and England. In France, Charles Faroux wrote: 'Personne, savant, technicien, praticien, pratiquant ou amateur, personne qui n'ait été attiré par ce chassis aux lignes pures, par cet ensemble si harmonieusement équilibré . . . . .' ('No one - technicians, drivers, car lovers or professionals - no one is not attracted by this chassis with its pure lines, the whole ensemble so harmoniously in equilibrium.') W.F. Bradley, the best motoring journalist of the time, gave a review of the H6 Hispano-Suiza in *The Autocar*, on 11 October 1919, which gives us all the facts in a straightforward and well-informed way. Throughout the twenties, the aero-engine continues to receive accolades, winning the World Altitude Record in 1923 and the same year Hispano's cars were 1, 2, 3 at the San Sebastian Grand Prix. The aero-engine continued its successful life, taking the World's Air Speed Record of 277.8 mph in Bonnet's Bernard Monoplane. This record was held for eight years, and in 1931 it took the World's straight line record as well.

Meanwhile the Rolls-Royce Silver Ghost, the 'Best Car in the World' was managing without four-wheel brakes, so the Marquis de Salamanca played the politest of tricks on Henry Royce, who was recuperating at Le Canadel after his overwork on the Hawk, the Eagle and the Falcon aero-engines. Salamanca had the Birkigt servo-assisted brakes fitted to the Countess of Prado-Amenos' Silver Ghost, and drove it round to see him and give him a convalescing ride in it. Royce agreed that Birkigt's brakes were indispensable and paid the patent fees to have all Rolls-Royces so fitted. Royce and A.J. Rowledge then improved them, of course, by changing the linkage.

Birkigt designed the Type 48, a four-cylinder version of the H6, a sensible car, one of which he gave to his daughter Yvonne when she was old enough, in 1929, and a car very popular in Spain

where it was used also as a military vehicle. T48s were made from 1924 to 1933.

During the twenties Dubonnet raced Hispanos successfully, having a well known tulip-wood sports car made by Nieuport, the aircraft people, and the 6.6-litre Hispano engine bored out to provide 8 litres. It managed only sixth in the 1924 Targa Florio, due to tyre problems, the engine and the driver deserving something better. This car is still alive and kicking. Dubonnet also won the Boillot cup at Boulogne and the Grand Prix at Monza with this car.

In 1924, Birkigt designed the T49 in Barcelona especially for Spain and the Spanish roads and people, and in 1928 he designed a pushrod six, for Hudson in the USA, with, at last, a single-plate clutch, but they had to reject it due to the infamous Wall Street Crash. A good car, it was produced in Spain as the Type 60 until 1943, despite the Spanish Revolution.

At this point it is important to realise the situation in Spain. Alfonso XIII is always the glittering figure in car literature; the splendid, helpful friend of Birkigt, a keen motorist with the world's first decent sports car named after him, and the owner not only of a dozen Hispanos, but later a Duesenberg. A hero figure, he was an outstanding tearaway of high society. But listen. Here are the facts. Born on 17 May 1886, he was the posthumous son of Alfonso XII, and immediately proclaimed King under the regency of Queen Maria Cristina, his doting Catholic mother. The atmosphere was ultra-clerical and he reacted against it as only a young Spaniard knew how. At sixteen years of age, he assumed full authority as King. Unprepared, dangerously mercurial, and constantly ill-advised, he

achieved a really magnificent political instability. There were 33 different governments between 1902 and 1923, until the parliamentary system was totally discredited.

Alfonso's popularity consequently suffered. There was an attempt on his life and that of his bride, Victoria Eugénie of Battenburg, on their wedding day, 31 May 1906, followed by a stream of attempts at assassination. Alfonso's undoubted personal courage won him admiration in face of these attacks. During the First World War, his conduct was straightforward, maintaining scrupulous neutrality. Alfonso had one burning objective: to rid himself of parliament altogether. He intervened in the Moroccan War in 1921, with horrific results. This was the time when Francisco Franco, another owner of several Hispanos over the years, was in one of his ascendancies. In command of the Spanish Foreign Legion, he brought the Moroccan Revolt to an end.

The course of Spanish history might have changed if Alfonso and Franco had worked together at this point, but Alfonso had a debt to another General, Miguel Primo de Rivera, who had rescued him from a humiliating series of awkward situations. When Rivera fell from power in 1930, a government under General Berenger was called in to save the King, but Alfonso had let things slide again, and in 1931 the people demanded his abdication. Alfonso refused, but the Army withdrew its support and the King had to leave Spain in a hurry, on 14 April 1931, in the very year when Birkigt was unveiling, at the Paris Show, the grandest car of all: the legendary Type T68 J12. Alfonso was there to see it. Where else to go?

There are far too few Hispanos about. Two hundred and sixty-two spread around the world is not enough, showing that life and reality has been exceptionally rough. Times have changed and I can remember the days when Hispanos were simply going about their business in the twenties and early thirties, driven by professional chauffeurs in tailored uniforms, characterized by quiet good manners, and a near religious devotion to their cars. As a boy, it was better to sit at the front beside this dedicated man whose conversation, should he speak, was more to the point than the weird mumbo-jumbo about politics and society in the back.

Birkigt had designed the Hispano-Suiza 'Junior' in 1930 and it was made in France with the T64 engine in a Ballot chassis with lowered frame. It did not sell well, however, being neither a proper Hispano nor an answer to real economy. In 1933 the K6, a splendid car, was unveiled at the Paris Show with a 5184 cc overhead valve, pushrod engine and a central gearchange. Manufactured until 1937, the price was from 100,000 to 120,000 francs. Birkigt's assistant at this time was Rudolph Hermann. In London, Hispano moved their showroom from Shaftesbury Avenue to 28 Albermarle Street, W1, an area more suitable, and I can remember a K6 drophead by Fernandez in the showroom. Hispano never had to face the Receiver, because Birkigt was not just one of the world's best engineers, he was an administrator, organiser, and a Director with vision. With two factories in Spain and another in France, he had a remarkably small board of directors. He was also aware that there would be a war sooner or later, so in 1932 he started developing the Hispano '404' cannon for use in aircraft. A friend of Burhle, the designer of the German Oerlikon cannon, Birkigt had actually been making it under licence for some time, and noticing ways in which it could be improved. He now began making his own model, and by 1939 he had delivered 90,000 '404' 20 mm cannon, to be fitted to fighter aircraft. Between 1935 and 1938 he also produced the 11-litre, Type 68 BIS 250 bhp at 3000 rpm and it was mainly used on the French railways, plus three cars.

Meanwhile, the Civil War in Spain had eliminated his truck factory at Guadalajara, the machine tools being removed and taken to Valencia by the Nationalists. The year 1936 was a bad one for Hispano, the Communist-inspired 'occupation of the factories' affecting Hispano as well as Bugatti, Delage and Delahaye.

In 1936, Léon Blum's government decided to nationalise all factories concerned with armaments, but Hispano-Suiza were given an exemption. At this time, Birkigt was concentrating completely on his 404 Cannon and gave control of the factories to: Jean Lacoste, Manager; Pierre Forgeot, Lawyer; and Maurice Heurteux, Director of Production. His son, Louis Birkigt, was in charge of aero-engine production.

Meanwhile, the fabulous parties of the rich continued from Paris to the Côte d'Azur, and by 1938, 120 Type 68 J12s had been delivered and were winning cups at the Concours d'Elégance, but car production ceased at Bois-Colombes. In 1938, the Hispano Type 12Y aero-engine was now delivering

HISPANO-SUIZA 68BIS

Vanvooren

an incredible 930 bhp and later, with fuel injection, 1,300 bhp, due largely to higher CR and metallurgy improvements, better bearings, etc. Birkigt was also engaged on the design of a V12 aero-engine.

When the Spanish Civil War ended in 1939, the Second World War commenced. During the 'cold war' period, a Hispano factory was opened at Janzac and when Paris fell, Birkigt moved his headquarters to Tarbes, but refused to collaborate with the Vichy Government. He found the atmosphere of collusion and confusion exasperating, so as a neutral citizen, he then decided to return to Barcelona, where he assisted with the Spanish Air Force, which was in a shambles at the time, due to the Civil War. Determined as ever to do something positive, he also designed a prototype, forward-control diesel truck, but when the Barcelona factories were sold in 1946, the Chief Engineer of Pegaso, Wilfred Ricart, who bought them, preferred naturally enough his own design to Birkigt's. His grandson, Marc-Louis Birkigt, was killed in an aviation accident around this time.

War over, Marshall Aid from America helped considerably to put Europe back on its feet and into production after the holocaust, but Hispano-Suiza received none, for two reasons. America did not welcome competition in aero-engine production, particularly from the best, and most of the Hispano-Suiza shareholders were Spanish, who, although neutral, had sometimes unforgivably sympathised with the Axis powers.

Birkigt was given a Grande Médaille d'Or by the Aero Club of France, and became a Grand Officer of the Légion d'honneur in 1945. Splendid.

But meanwhile it was goodbye to the Guadalajara factories, devastated by the Civil War, goodbye to the Barcelona factories, sold to Pegaso trucks, and a sad farewell to Bois-Colombes where all the cars shown here, some of the best in the world, were made, as well as an aero-engine almost miraculous in quality. Marc Birkigt himself died in 1953, of cancer, at his villa at Versoix. Only a few friends attended the funeral.

There is complete unanimity about Marc Birkigt the man. Dedicated to his work at all times, he designed everything which bore the name Hispano-Suiza. He willingly delegated administrative matters, and gave latitude to those in which he had confidence, but never in matters of design and engineering. Courteous always, but with no jokes or satire, no familiarities whatsoever, and no explosions of rage. His reserve was more or less impregnable; inhuman even. He amassed a considerable fortune, but it did not change his way of life in the slightest. He was not working to become rich, he became wealthy because his work was unique and impeccable. The complete removal of all his factories like some wind blowing away his footsteps in the sand, did not cancel out the fantastic cars, 262 of which still remain, with the same fire, integrity and refinement, which they were so noted for fifty years ago. Compare their statistics with the other best cars in the world. Better still, buy one and drive it.

Overleaf: HISPANO-SUIZA J12, 1934
unknown coachbuilder.

6

BUGATTI

& Ettore

Bugattis encapsulate concepts of engineering which, once seen, change your ideas radically and definitively. Drive them, and you realise that each car is form and engineering in equilibrium, and a work of art. They are scarce, pricey, and becoming more so annually, so you may never have that pleasure unless you are phenomenally successful and lucky as well.

Ettore himself was quite a man. *'Le style est l'homme'* fitted him just as well as it did Napoleon. By this I mean not the bowler, breeches and Irish Hunter, but the real life style of Bugatti *at work*, the creative vortex of engineering surrounded by anonymous craftsmen and engineers, working incomparably as a team.

In the late twenties and thirties Bugatti meant avant garde, but it also stood for thoroughbred. In fact the Bugatti Owners Club was one of the most select societies in France, concerned with style, and also an intoxication with speed. It had a dark side, concerned with latent self-destruction also. After a night in the bar at La Coupole, a Viennese dancer, Lena Amsel, who owned a 'Buga', challenged André Derain the painter, another member of the BOC, to a race. She was burned alive after turning hers over. Louis Aragon and Max Ernst - she had lived with both - were at the funeral and all Montmartre was furious with André Derain for causing the death of a girl who had all the qualities a female needs and more. At this time a best seller was *De La Vitesse* by Paul Morand, who owned several Bugattis. 'Women,' he said in this book, 'were fascinated by men whose

personalities centred around the hectic rhythm of Bugatti engines. Paris mechanics were not good enough for these devotees; at the least alarm at a change of engine note, they raced off to Molsheim, which they entered as a temple, and if luck was with them, may meet Ettore himself, 'Le Patron', or better still, stay at his small hotel.'

You may find all this adulation scarcely credible, but not when it is remembered that one particular Bugatti model won 1045 races in two years, and one sports car set up a speed record which stood for twenty years.

The hub of the Bugatti miracle was that Ettore not only designed the cars but that he set up at Molsheim a unique factory system - a mix of Rolls-Royce perfectionism plus Ferrari passion. This was a factory not only with the best craftsmen and machine tools, it was a complex of co-ordinated talents all chosen by Ettore Bugatti and working with him, his hand on every pulse, driving around on that tiller steered go-kart.

It was inevitable that Molsheim would perish when Bugatti died, because the only person who could have kept it alive, Jean (Gianoberto) Bugatti, was killed in 1939.

Car firms are now supported by massive capital investment and often by state support as well. Bugatti succeeded single-handed. This success was based on two crucial factors. The first one was the organic unity of Bugatti classics, engine, suspension, transmission, steering and braking systems. The second was the integrity of materials and workmanship. Bugatti stated his simple but impeccable credo to *L'Auto* the French magazine in 1927. 'My racing cars are production models, like my sports cars. Even the tourers have the same engine and mechanisms as my racing cars, built with the same materials and assembled by the same workmen.' With such a kernel it is no surprise that the cars were fabulously successful then, and gilt-edged securities now.

Fate had to be helping surely. The Bugatti story, like a Greek myth, has success and multiple tragedies inextricably intermingled from beginning to end. At seventeen, Ettore raced motorized trikes, rejecting the idea of following his father and brother into the art business. 'My ideas give me no rest' he kept saying, as he dismantled his de Dion Bouton engine and improved it, winning yet more races. The Biscaretti Motor Museum in Turin, one of the very best in the world, has archives telling us that on

12 March 1899, on a Prinetti and Stucchi trike with de Dion Bouton engine, Ettore won the 100-mile race from Verona to Mantua. He was in august company. Count Biscaretti, founder of the museum, was second, Fraschini third, and Agnelli, later to be founder of Fiat, first in the car class.

It was not all racing. There was romance; not with some rambling rose of the wild wood, but with a creature straight out of Homer. Listen carefully. Ettore's mother and her best friend got married in the same month. They both had babies, also in the same month the next year, and the mothers often swapped babies for a while. Ettore Bugatti and Barbara Mascherpa Bolsoni were these two babies. Naturally they had an affinity deeper than normal. Later they married, becoming engaged when Ettore won his medal at Milan for the best prototype car.

Their first daughter L'Ébé (EB pronounced French style) was born before the marriage. Barbara Bugatti had all the qualities: beauty, elegance, wit, a consoler, an advisor, and a scintillating hostess at the Bugatti marquees on the racing circuits where she organised champagne, caviare and pigeon salads. The mother of L'Ébé, Lydia, Jean and Roland, she was also an inspiration at all times, but sadly gets little billing in the Bugatti saga, not even in *The Bugatti Story* written by daughter L'Ébé.

As inexorable as a centrifuge, fate set about turning Bugatti into a genius. First, it excited him about engineering by winning trike races, then provided him with this fabulous mate. Next, to broaden his horizons; for the small Bugatti home, No 13 Via Marconi might warp him. So Dominique Lamberjack was conjured up, to take young Ettore on a lengthy tour of France and Italy, learning about engines, racing cars, and life in general. Lamberjack was in the car business, buying and selling.

Bugatti had listened to some lectures by Count Enrico Bernardi, professor of maths and engineering at Padova University. From the heterogeneous experience of this period and his exceptional intuition, but no formal education in engineering whatsoever, Bugatti made a car between 1899 and 1900. He made it in every sense of the word, with his own hands. He produced drawings, wooden patterns, superintended the making of castings and forgings, and then fitted the parts together. So far so good. But to leap from that first car to the fabulous Bugattis which were to dominate the European Grand Prix, and turn the Targa Florio

into a Bugatti procession, like that of Porsches at Le Mans, asked a lot of Lady Luck.

Fate set up six springboards, each with a lot of thrust, to get him there.

1) The first Bugatti won a silver cup at the 1901 Milan Motor Show for the best prototype, Fiat winning the major prize for the best production car.

2) Fate organized that Baron Eugen de Dietrich should be at the Milan Show and Bugatti whispered, hot and fiercely into his ear that he was the man the Baron needed as chief engineer of the Alsace side of his firm. The Baron could hardly refuse, and Bugatti learned a great deal more than he gave at Dietrich, about machine tools and practicalities.

3) When Bugatti left de Dietrich he set up as an engineer designer on the top floor of the Hotel de Paris, in Graffenstaden, and Fate sat right down beside him. Between them they produced the Hermes car for Mathis, a four-cylinder ohc engine for Deutz, and some say the ohc engine for Fiat, which won the 1911 French Grand Prix.

4) Deutz invited Ettore Bugatti to be chief engineer on the strength of the engine he had designed for them. While Fate was helping Ettore, Madame Bugatti had two daughters and carried on long demanding conversations with her small statue of the Virgin Mary, turning her face to the wall when her suggestions were not fulfilled. Bugatti was now 23. The engines he designed for Deutz were like heavy-weight ancestors to subsequent Bugattis and he was only too aware that they were not right. His ideas were giving him no rest, as usual.

5) While his wife was pregnant with Jean, a time when men are often creative, Ettore worked long hours every night in the cellar of their house in Cologne, when he built the first *Pur-sang*. 'This is it,' he pronounced, 'we are off' (better in French). Fate again, caused the Deutz directors to break their contact with Bugatti, and give him 20,000 Reichmarks for so doing. A useful sum. An open body was quickly made for the *Pur Sang* and it was driven to Strasbourg by Ettore, with madame and the children. This almost sacred car was found in a breaker's yard in Bordeaux in 1950. Another Bugatti, a 5-litre which Ettore Bugatti had made at Deutz, was driven to Strasbourg by Ernest Friderich, his lifelong helper and friend. This is 'Black Bess', still in existence, and now beyond price.

6) Fate now went ahead and got to work on Count de Vizcaya, head of the Darmstadt Bank, who

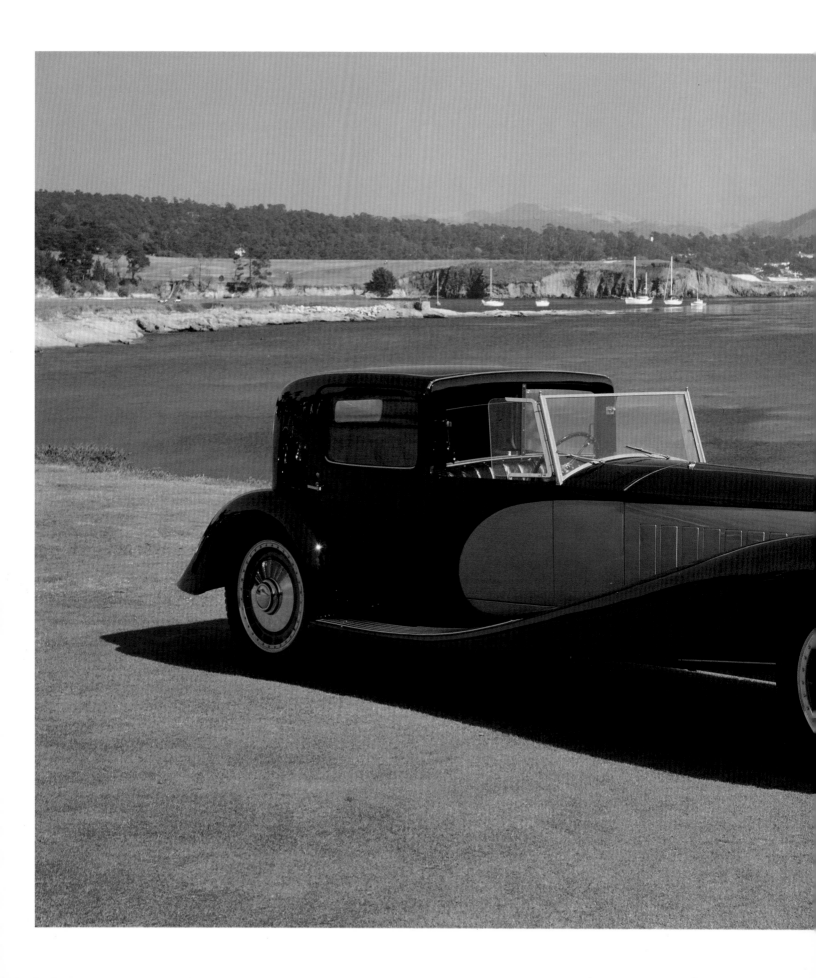

BUGATTI T41 ROYALE

Bugatti

made friends with Bugatti, loaned him money, and suggested Molsheim Dye Works as a suitable factory.

Bugatti now really got moving. The dye works were white-washed and the family set up in a house next to it, just before Christmas 1909. By January 1910 the machine tools arrived, and by the end of the year, five Type 13s had been made, with a staff of 20. Each car had been tested for 600 miles and carried a 5-year guarantee. The next year, Friderich drove a Type 13 to second place at Le Mans. It was a long way behind the big Fiat, driven by Victor Hemery, but Ettore had designed that one also, according to the real devotees of Ettore Bugatti. That same year, 1911, he designed the world's archetypal baby car, the type BP1 Bébé for Peugeot; showing remarkable prescience in several respects. To round off that year he patented his classic reversed quarter-elliptic rear suspension system (patent 21160). A vintage year.

W. F. Bradley wrote a brilliant article in *The Motor* 1 Nov 1910, the first description of a Molsheim car, so he was the first to appreciate and help Birkigt, Delage and Bugatti.

Ettore Bugatti had now not only produced a new breed of car, but a method of creating more. Molsheim had all the creative organisation and machinery put together like a magic beehive. Craftsmen in all necessary fields worked together, sharing specialist knowledge and relating details to the basic concept. Ettore Bugatti was 'Le Patron' because they respected his design ability, craftsmanship and spirit. They were also contented in their work and proud of the product. They had won a second at Le Mans, first shot.

Above: BUGATTI T41, 1932, Kellner.

Without this team, Ettore Bugatti was nowhere near so good, as we can see from the weird 16-cylinder aero-engine which he produced during the war, when he was alone.

Finally, Bugatti showed an insight into the psychology of merchandising which was just as advanced as the cars. The only people who could afford Bugattis were the rich, who had the good taste to recognise quality and also delight in speed, but who were, in the main, uninterested in engineering complexities. The last thing they wanted to hear, was the whirring of the Bugatti brain. So Ettore put on a bowler hat and breeches, and mounted his thoroughbred, which, so they say, gives instant nobility. It certainly limits thought and conversation. A collection of carriages as well as a museum of small arms, including cross-bows, flint- and match-locks, Winchesters and Colts, provided interests for his visiting customers, and there was also a small hotel run by Madame Bugatti. His friend Dominique Lamberjack looked after the traded-in Alvis, Bentley, Talbot, Daimler, and Delaunay-Belleville limousines.

Everyone was charmed with the Molsheim Renaissance concept. They admired the distillery making Mirabelle liqueur, the landscaped gardens, and the bronze hinges to the factory doors through

BUGATTI T43

Bugatti

which they NEVER passed. Beyond these doors was a form of high technology which would have been incomprehensible to them. In a dust-free, white-painted environment, some of the best engineers in the world were silently fitting engines and chassis impeccably together, with the simplest machine tools, perfection as their objective. They were also using the special Bugatti-patented nuts and bolts with various threads, and integral washers.

Customers gone, Ettore's bowler was off, and he was back with those ideas which gave him no rest. And his men. One afternoon a week was devoted to the personal problems of his team - ill health, money, or family worries. 'The New Renaissance' they called Molsheim, but such humanity was something which Guilliano de Medici never considered to be the duty of a Prince. There were 400 working with Bugatti in 1914, in this kind of harmony and understanding.

The First World War was a tragedy to all Europe and everyone in it. To Ettore Bugatti it meant closing Molsheim, which was his life. He moved to Milan and later to Paris, where he designed a good straight-eight aero-engine of 250 bhp. He then designed a 16-cylinder aero-engine for the Americans. There is a model of it in the Musée de l'Air at Chalais-Meudon near Paris. Look at it and decide for yourself; I think it was a mistake.

War over, Molsheim was in need of a clean up. The old craftsmen returned delightedly to work, but they needed pay, and the factory had to have new materials. Money, which is something the specialist biographers never mention, was obtained by Bugatti himself, sometimes designing for other car manufacturers. That year, he sold designs to Crossley, Isotta-Fraschini and Panhard he also designed the Type 35 which, after a period of multiple modifications, began a seven-year domination of the car circuits, with beauty thrown in.

Although Bugattis were an art form unbedevilled by advertisements Ettore knew the value of advertising, and rounded off 1926 with an advertisement in *Revue Automobile*.

BUGATTI
du 24 janvier 1926
au 19 septembre
501
VICTOIRES
Plus de 14 victoires par semaine
47 records - 351 fois premier
Parmi lesquelles
CHAMPIONNAT DU MONDE
Targea Florio 1, 2, 3
GP de Rome 1
GP d'Alsace 1, 2, 3
GP d'Espagne 1, 2
GP d'Europe 1, 2
GP de Boulogne 1, 2
GP d'Italie 1, 2
GP de Milan 1, 2, 3
GP de France 1, 2

That longing for the fabulous which coloured Bugatti's existence, had several flowerings. The racing cars were one, but he had another: to produce a car suitable for Emperors. After the height of racing

82   BUGATTI T44, 1929, Bugatti.

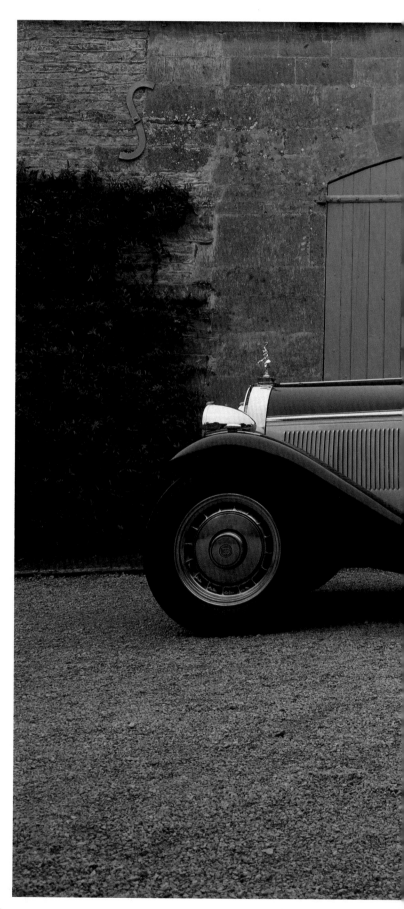

success in 1926 he made a prototype, No 41, which he enjoyed driving all over Europe, often at 120 mph. The chassis and engine were camouflaged by a Packard tourer body. The straight-eight engine, of 12,763 cc, was one of the most important engines developed by Bugatti. The water-jackets did not stop conventionally with the cylinders, but ran on to cool the crankshaft and crankcase, making an architectural monobloc. The crankshaft, with circular webs, was carried in nine plain bearings. The valves, two inlet and one exhaust, were operated via two scavenge and one feed pump. Double ignition was by coil and dynamo. Separate from the engine and actually under the driver's seat, was the flywheel and clutch. The gearbox was situated with the final drive as a transaxle.

The guarantee of the Royale was for the lifetime of the owner. Only six Royales were made, royalty being on the decline. The Type 41 engine were consequently adapted for the first rail 'Automotrices', where they set up new records, of 124mph. These engines were in service until 1958, and represent another Bugatti original idea. The 'TGV' runs between Paris and Lyon daily at 168 mph.

A hair crack appeared in the impeccable Bugatti empire in 1936. The Depression had brought a resurgence of union activity of such venom that the workers prevented Bugatti from entering his own factory at Molsheim. Actually the work force had been considerably increased to cope with the rail project and it was this element, of the recently arrived, which was rebellious. Ettore immediately left Molsheim, and set up a design office over the Bugatti showrooms in the Avenue Montaigne in Paris. Jean, his son, was left in control at Molsheim, supervising the railway project, motor racing, and the Type 57 sports car.

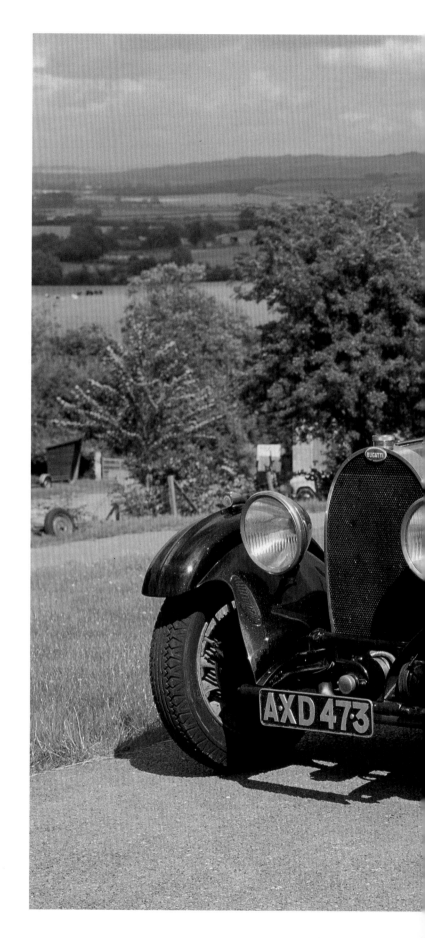

BUGATTI T55

Jean Bugatti

There were union troubles again in 1937 but Jean got the ban lifted in time to prepare a car which not only won the Le Mans at 82.126 mph, but also secured the Index of Performance. This was repeated in 1939, raising the speed to 86.856 mph. Jean was also driving the 'Automotrice' with the Type 41 engines and setting new world speed records for rail travel.

Bugatti had forbidden Jean to race in competition, but he often used to test drive the cars on a stretch of road near the factory. This road was closed on these occasions, but in August 1939, although the foreman closed it at one end, young Roland, Jean's kid brother, could not persuade the laughing, bicycling postman to stop. Jean was driving on peak revs, took avoiding action, rolled the car and was killed. The postman later committed suicide. The death of Jean was the main reason for the final collapse of the Bugatti enterprise. Fate was starting to take to pieces the wonderful Bugatti mythology which it had built up completely, the humans as well as the buildings.

The Second World War was a lethal demolition machine. The Germans used Molsheim to produce torpedos, and redesigned the factory for the purpose. War over, the Canadians came and had an enormous accidental fire. The Americans were next, and mislaid papers, drawings and machine tools, alike. Total chaos.

BUGATTI T51, 1933, Bugatti.

BUGATTI T57C

Letourneur et Marchand

Madame Bugatti meanwhile, originally the inspiration and part of the spirit, was dying of cancer. She was buried on 21 July 1944. Ettore had been living with Geneviève Delcuze with whom he had two children, and they now married. But Ettore died on 21 August 1947, worn out by a life at peak revs, and the renewed strain of legal proceedings necessary to regain Molsheim after the war.

So there were now six heirs to the estate. Roland, Lydia, and L'Ébé, and Geneviève Delcuze and her two children. Molsheim was a corpse and no more magical cars would come out of it.

There was only one thing left to be done. Someone must be inspired to collect all the Bugattis together for posterity, and as an inspiration to future engineers.

1936
BUGATTI T57
Atalante, Jean Bugatti

Fate chose Fritz Schlumpf to fulfil this useful objective. He had already started a small collection in one of his factory buildings at Mulhouse. He was, after all, the sixth richest man in France and could afford a collection of classic cars. This was not good enough for Fate, who turned Fritz into a near madman, with an uncontrollable obsession to buy *all* the Bugattis.

He bought whole collections if there were four of five Bugattis in them. Goods trains came into Mulhouse from all over Europe, loaded with

vintage cars, and of course Schlumpf and his brother became bankrupt. The workers at his textile factory rebelled. Fritz Schlumpf's wife, who lived in Paris, shot her Greek lover because he would not move out to let in Fritz. The Paris newspapers were in ecstasies. Fate had succeeded magnificently. One hundred and twenty two Bugattis were all in one museum.

A consortium bought the whole collection, which is now named *Musée Nationale de l'Automobile*. Mulhouse has a whole complex of museums, one of them being the French Railway museum, which of course has an example of the Automotrice with the Type 41 engines. Few, if any, marques have been so comprehensively collected together.

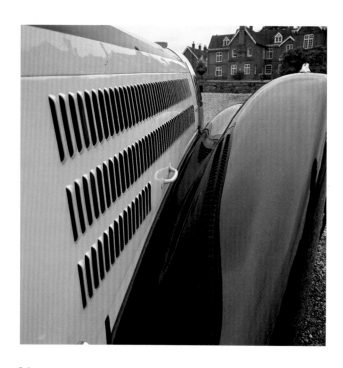

1936
BUGATTI T57
Ventoux, Jean Bugatti

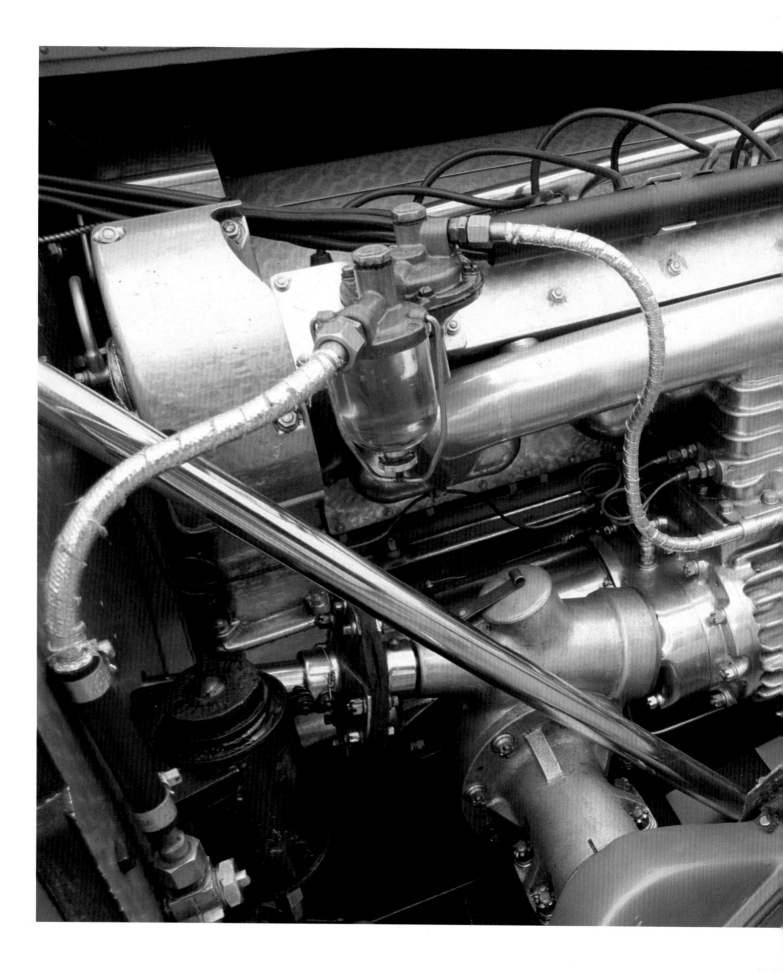

7

DELAGE

Louis de l'Age d'Or

L ouis Delage created an important part of the tradition and heritage of the automotive golden age in France. Delage cars have all that is meant by '*La belle voiture français*', together with Bugattis, Hispano-Suiza and, later, Talbot-Lago, which inspired France's coachbuilders to produce moving works of art. The spirit and personal taste of Louis Delage was a constant factor in determining the entire Delage *oeuvre*, from engine and chassis to the particular kind of coachwork, and in this respect it must be realised that even his early runabouts had flair when he designed them himself.

His life was purposeful from the start. He had not only vision, but the ability to accomplish it. Later of course, he borrowed the life style of his richest customers and, at its peak, he had a château, a town house and a yacht. Born in Cognac, France, in 1874, the son of a station master, he attended the École des Arts et Métiers at Angers, graduating as an engineer in 1895. After military service in Algeria, he moved to Paris in 1900 and set up as a consultant engineer. In 1903 he became chief draughtsman-engineer at Peugeot, and resigned two years later, at 31, to found Delage et Cie, taking Augustin Legros, another engineer, with him. Legros had been trained at Cluny, also in an Arts et Métiers college. One of the central themes in Delage is that with only one exception, all the engineers had received their training in these colleges and they were aware of it, like a brotherhood, calling each other 'Gadzarts'. They had another celebrated brother in Marc Birkigt, who was trained at the Arts et Métiers College at Geneva. The first Delage hot-house was one room on the fifth floor of 62 Rue Chaptal, Levallois. It is a small world. Bugatti designed the straight-eight and V16 aero-engines at No. 86. The French car industry was beginning quietly, like this, in small design offices.

Delage and Legros started this marque in 1905. Thirty years later, they were still together, Legros in command of the production, Louis Delage of concepts and financial management. In June 1905 they rented a barn at 83, Rue Anatole France, where they started to make the first prototypes. They had four lathes, a drill and a milling machine. For the Salon de l'Auto in Paris in December 1905, they produced three cars, all with de Dion Bouton engines, but with Delage and Legros ideas on suspension and transmission - and a dashing style. Charles Faroux, the most important motoring journalist in France at that time, gave the cars such a good write-up in *L'Echo des Sports* that there were many orders. Also, a wealthy man interested in the new industry loaned Louis 150,000 francs with the condition that his son should be employed at Delage, so a larger place was rented at 2 Place du General Leclerc, and Louis designed and built two voiturettes there, one of which came second in the Coupe des Voiturettes de *L'Auto*. The winner was a Sizaire et Naudin. Lion Peugeots were third and fourth. Bugatti had a second at le Mans with his Type 13, similarly, and in both cases, racing produced publicity. Delage at the Salon that year received still more capital from eager businessmen wishing to obtain dealerships in Delage cars.

In 1907 Delage bought an acre of land in Levallois, including an empty hangar of a building. Everything was moved into it and the other premises vacated. During 1907 the director of a machine tool firm invested a substantial sum in Delage. He remained the main stockholder, and a friend, until 1935.

In 1908, Delage produced three cars for the Grand Prix des Voitures at Dieppe, and they came in 1st, 5th and 12th. This result, against international competition, produced so many orders that a new building was erected of over 20,000 sq ft which meant that Delage now had almost an acre under cover. Louis had a splendid idea on how to use the space. He made a deal with Ballot of real consequence, including the following: (a) Ballot to provide 50% of Delage needs. (b) Drawings, jigs and tools to be provided so that Delage could produce the same engines. (c) All engines to have Delage nameplate. So much for engines.

Next, he turned those interesting eyes, one curiously still, the other vibrant, to coachwork. He persuaded François Repusseau, who had set up as a coachbuilder, with a blacksmith, a joiner and an upholsterer, to produce coachbuilt bodies for 250 francs each. Legros used to grumble about this sharp practice in the market place. They were worth double that amount.

Arthur-Léon Michelat (Arts et Métiers, Angers) became chief engineer in 1909, leaving Legros to look after production, and the next year Demolliens (Arts et Métiers, Lille) became technical assistant and secretary.

So far, the gears had been bought from Malicet-Blin, but Delage had a compulsion, like Henry Royce, to make everything himself and buy-in nothing. Maurice Gaultier (Arts et Métiers, Lille) was in charge of gears, until later when he designed engines including the fabulous D8. Sales were so spectacular and profitable now, it was necessary to obtain larger premises, and in Paris, so, 60 Boulevard Perière Nord was acquired as a service and spares centre, together with administration offices.

In 1936, it became law for workers in France to have one week of paid holiday a year. Delage had pre-empted this by no less than a quarter of a century, on the basis of one day per year of employment with the company. Sales kept increasing and the workforce was contented. New premises were required again, and were built at Courbevoie, next to Hispano-Suiza. In the considerable information about Delage and his life there is no record of his ever meeting Birkigt at Hispano-Suiza. Yet they must have seen each other there, and at the Salons, constantly. Different men, poles apart.

Gaultier became production manager of the Courbevoie factory, with new designs for engines, no longer Ballot influenced. (Hispano-Suiza then bought up Ballot.)

So far, the success of Delage had been made with small four-cylinder cars, up to 2 litres in capacity. In 1913, he produced the Type AH, a 2.5-litre six, starting his movement towards the smoothness required for the luxury market.

The 1914-18 war had less effect on Delage than Bugatti. The Courbevioe plant was ordered to make munitions and shells, which it did for the duration. Gaultier sadly was imprisoned for criminally faulty manufacture of these items, being un-interested. He had concerned himself, together with Michelat, with the 17 CV six, which was to be made in peace-time, as the Type 'Co'. As they

1924

DELAGE CO2

Delage

could not make it in the shell and munitions area, Louis Delage set up a machine shop in the old Perein factory, calling it 'Ateliers Mécaniques À Réfrigier'. The Type 'Co' prototype was ready in 1917 and actually used by the army as staff cars, Fregal escure (Arts et Métiers, Aix-en-Provence) joining, to help produce a hundred of them.

DELAGE DM

Labourdette

War over, and straining at the leash to get started producing his new six, Louis Delage himself, very macho, drove a Type 'Co', with W. F. Bradley as a witness again for the British AA, from Paris to Nice at the high average of 41.5 mph over frightful roads, and the side-valve 'Co' was no thunderbird. It was presented at the first post-war Paris Salon in 1919, together with a poster showing Louis at the wheel on his Paris-Nice record run.

There is something of a shadow hovering over Louis at this point. He had become wealthy before the war by his capacities as a brilliant engineer, but he became even more wealthy during the war, which is a different kettle of fish. Armaments paid too well. He bought a huge town house, No. 140 Boulevard des Champs Elysées, and transformed it into a suitably grand setting for a marque which

would shortly be *grande classe*. It was more elegant than any other. Personally, he had a chateau at Le Pecq, a villa at Saint-Briac, a townhouse at 42, Avenue du Bois, and a magnificent ocean yacht, *L'Oasis*. Sales of the Type 'Co', however, were really sluggish, meanwhile. Throughout its entire run, 1917-21, only 1390 were made, despite its obviously sound, well-engineered production, and four-wheel brakes. So Delage set off again around France, accompanied by Bradley again, this time for a 3,120 mile belt in six days, but still no one wanted the Type 'Co'. So he made the Type 'Do', a four-cylinder version of the 'Co', which sold even less: only 212. In 1919 another engineer was appointed, Charles Planchon (Arts et Métiers, Angers), who was actually Louis' cousin. Working with Escure, they produced the four-cylinder L-head, Type 'DE', ready for the 1921 Salon: by 1923 it had sold 3,600. Sighs of relief, and praise for Planchon.

As hundreds of unsold side valve Type 'Co' were still taking up factory space, the engine was redesigned for overhead valves operated by pushrods, It then gave 80 instead of 65 bhp. This was now the 'Co2' and no one liked it either, so only 200 of the old 'Co' were transformed to 'Co2' and that was the end of that. The ohv 'Co2' is a splendid, heroic vehicle; the public, as is quite often the case, were wrong: it was a dog with a bad name.

Nineteen twenty-two marked the return of Delage to sports cars, designed by Henri Toutée (trained at Chenard et Walcker), these being the types DIE, DISS, DIS. Altogether 938 were made and much admired by the collectors; frisky, pleasant to drive and flexible.

The like poles syndrome between father and son now occurred, and young Pierre Delage set off for Tangiers, Morocco, with a rage in the grand manner. Everyone saw that Louis was mean to him. He expected blind obedience, but Pierre could only provide defiance. This was 1923. After running a garage in Morocco and a year with Amilcar, Pierre returned in 1929. It would appear that he was not in the same class as Jean Bugatti, but an engineer nonetheless.

The three years, 1923, 4 and 5, were financial growth years. In 1923 Louis made the firm into a public company, with a capital of a million francs. During the following year, this became 5 million and the next year, 25 million. Louis, meanwhile, was smouldering over the idea of a supercar to be better than the Hispano-Suiza, made

literally next door. He had met Maurice Sainturat (Arts et Métiers, Angers) and admired a prototype which he had designed for Hotchkiss. Sainturat demanded liberty, absolute autonomy, and huge salary. He produced a highly polished lame duck, the GL. It was delicate, unimaginably complex, with a weakness in the drive to the overhead camshafts. Two hundred GLs were made, but the demand was much less than that. Sainturat left, and Louis fired his cousin Planchon as well. There was trouble also in the main Delage factory, with the type D1, which turned out to be under-powered and not in demand. Escure, who had designed it, gave up engineering altogether to grow grapes in Bordeaux, due to Louis' dark hate. Gaultier had also left during one of Louis' rages. Legros, the calm peace-maker, now invited him back in 1925. He set about Escure's D1, and turned it into a gem, and also designed the Type DM, a six-cylinder version of the D1, which produced twice as much brake horsepower as the four-cylinder car. By 1927 he had designed and produced the Type DR, which sold 5,400 in two years, largely because it was very reliable, with no faults at all.

Albert Lory (Arts et Métiers, Angers) had, at an enormous cost, designed the $1\frac{1}{2}$-litre racing car which, in 1927, won the Grand Prix World Championship, not the subject of this book, which is concerned with limousines, but the success produced fabulous sales of all models; 3,000 in that year. At this time there were 2,000 employees. The factory had many similarities with Molsheim: Good design and finesse everywhere, including the very best machine tools.

Outside, the huge Depression was on its way, but Delage was serene in its magnificence on the Champs Elysées. The 1929 Salon showed the splendid D8, 4-litres with 105 bhp, smooth, silent, elegant and luxurious, Maurice Gaultier's high-water mark of excellence. There is one feature in particular which places the D8 among the great cars of all time, and this is the overall high standard of engineering - there are no faults at all. The gearbox, for example, is outstandingly good, due to Gaultier's specialization for years in this field. This thoroughbred of engineering was given outstanding coachwork by Chapron, Figoni, Letourneur et Marchand, Saoutchik, Labourdette, Vanden Plas, Freestone & Webb, Barker, Pourtout, Fernandez & Darrin; they *all* wanted to show what they could do with it.

Two sizes, the DS and the D6, both derived from the D8, were introduced in 1930, after the Wall Street crash. A bad year, with 2000 cars built, but many unsold. Desperately, a front wheel drive prototype was designed and made, with despair and confusion everywhere, but especially in Louis' mind and troubled spirit.

Nineteen thirty-two was worse than ever, but Louis Delage received a bank loan of 25 million francs, heaven knows how at such a time. Albert Lory designed and they made a prototype of a supercharged, V12 aero-engine, which was shown at the Salon de l'Aéronautique, but this one-off prototype was involved in an accident which completely demolished it. With this, it was 'back to the wall' in 1933. Louis sold the Champs Elysées building and everything went back to Courbevoie. Gaultier worked to some purpose and designed a D6 11, a new D4, and the tremendous straight-eight D8 15, but they all had the same faults as those made by manufacturers with insufficient resources: gearboxes and final drives were common to all of them, and therefore right only for one.

Morale sank low. In 1933, Delage offered the firm to Robert Peugeot and he refused. This was no surprise. What would Peugeot, concerned with racing and the mass market, but restraint in everything, do with the Delage Empire? He offered it to Gnome et Rhône, and they agreed to pay 100 million francs for the assets and the name. Madame Delage, however, had some connection with this transaction and she refused. Her marriage settlement was tied up with the firm and Louis was notoriously unfaithful. She was being awkward. Rumours of disaster were everywhere, and debts were enormous.

Then Michelat returned and designed the D6/65, D8/85 and D8/195 and they were all on show at the Salon in 1934. There were many orders for all of these models, but it was too late. There was no capital even for the materials to make them.

In April 1935 the Receiver took over. The Delage name was to continue after the liquidation. Walter Watney bought the assets for 2 million francs (a fraction of their worth) and arranged for Delahaye to assemble the cars, and make them also. Finally Watney sold his Delage assets to Delahaye completely.

After the deluge, the following events took place:
(a) The Delage showrooms in the Champs Elysées were taken over by Ford in 1936, and later by Simca. Exit Routières. Enter cars for everyman.

Page 126: DELAGE D8N, 1932, Fernandez. **123**

128

(b) In 1938 the Delahaye-engined D8 120 became the supreme queen of the Concours d'élégance, much to purist Delageists' annoyance.

(c) Louis Delage set off on a walking pilgrimage to Chartres, and then to Lourdes on a bicycle.

(d) Paul Yvelin, for many years an employee at Delage, met Louis Delage on the Champs-Elysées near No. 140, looking very shabby and with broken spectacles, staring at the Fords in his old showroom. Louis Delage died in 1947 aged 73. Madame Delage, blind, died in 1970.

There are several pictures of Delages here, and they show the quality which pervades their design throughout engines and coachwork. Formal, dignified, they tolerate no softness. They brought dignity and integrity with them everywhere; even the febrile concours d'élégances with the owners' wives wearing curious expressions, moulded on their faces by hours of tedium, waiting for their turn to be photographed, waiting for their number to be called out, to be inspected, waiting anxiously for the results to be read out.

There are critics who find a curious atavism in the design of this Routière's engine, completely disregarding Albert Lory's classic racing engine, but the D8 was not designed for rally-type driving over sinuous country roads or hairpin bends in the Alps. It is the classic Grande Routière, perfect for the long white *routes nationales* of France. Delage completely disagreed with the Bugatti and Talbot-Lago formula of the same engine for monoposto, sports car and Routière.

Louis Delage believed from the beginning in the value of racing. His laurels included the 1908 GP des Voiturettes, 1911 Light car GP of Boulogne, 1913 GP of France, 1914 Indianapolis, 1925 French and Spanish GPs, 1927 World Championship, 1928 Brooklands 200 mile race, 1931 Dieppe Voiturettes, 1932 Avus 1500cc GP, 1933 Eifelrennen and the 1936 Prix de Berne Switzerland, among many others. Also, among the great number of racing cars ever produced, the 1926/27 1½-litre straight-eight Delage designed by Albert Lory stands out like a milestone, winning every major race it contested in 1927 and, *ipso facto*, taking the World Championship. It had cost a great deal, however, and Delage showed a surprising new side to his flamboyant character, of restraint, by giving up racing while he was winning. On the crest of the wave, he sold his beautiful cars in 1927. Malcolm Campbell got one, and Earl Howe

DELAGE D6 3-LITRE

Chapron

acquired two, one of which, sadly, was written off against a tree at Monza. Dick Seaman bought the other one from Earl Howe and Giulio Ramponi raised the power to 185 bhp from 165 by increasing the blower pressure. In 1936, Seaman won the RAC 1½-litre race on the Isle of Man, against nine modern ERAs. One original GP Delage survives.

Despite this success in racing, Louis Delage believed that Routières required a different engine altogether from those which had, at enormous cost, won races. The Routières required engines with more torque at low revs, and the ability to move two tons of luxury smoothly and in silence, and that is what he got, in the D8. The D6, which had some features in common with the D8, however, was second at the 1939 Le Mans - to a Bugatti 57 - and again second in 1949 - to a Ferrari 166 MH.V12. This accounts for the current increasing popularity of the 3-litre Delage D6.

It is very depressing that Louis Delage, who had been so successful in so many fields, should not only end in bankruptcy, but personal poverty and distress as well. Meanwhile, the factory at Levallois, from which he moved to Courbevoie when the going was good, was sold to Meunier the chocolate people, who have continued to be commercially successful. What a difference from Delage's despair and failure after years of effort in

Above: DELAGE D8 120, 1938, Letourneur et Marchand.

DELAGE D8 120

Chapron

a high tech area. Chocolate making is apparently more profitable than engineering and less risky.

Paul Yvelin, the authority on Delage history, wrote his *Notes et Souvenirs* and had them published at his own expense, because he was worried that the Delage epic might 'slide into oblivion', as the man had done. This did not happen. Those with an eye for form, a mind for engineering and a recognition of quality have preserved Delages, restored to perfection. At present their prices are low compared with Bugatti, but they have potential and in ten years' time they will have doubled at the auctions.

The oldest single-marque club in Europe, *Les Amis de Delage*, meet regularly to discuss maintenance and restoration problems. They will last for ever, more or less, these examples of French art and engineering. Park one before any château and it instantly becomes part of the scene, and 'La Gloire'.

8

DELAHAYE

& three engineers

Bugatti cars were created by Ettore Bugatti; Hispano-Suizas by Marc Birkigt; Delages by Louis Delage and his engineers, the 'Gadzarts'; Talbot-Lagos were created by Anthony Lago, and, in each case, one single-minded engineer. Delahaye had three men, over the years, who were responsible for Delahayes, with remarkably varied characteristics and qualities. From, 1895 to 1905, Emile Delahaye himself designed the cars and also drove in competitions. The cars were simple, with both strength and quality. Emile drove one in the 1896 Paris-Marseilles-Paris, and it is still to be seen at Le Mans, in the museum there. In 1901 Emile retired due to ill health, and in 1906 he died. Charles Weiffenbach then became Director, and remained there as 'Monsieur Charles' until the firm disappeared in 1954. He died in 1959. His first chief engineer, M. Varlet, designed an engine named 'Titan' which was used in large, heavy saloons and tourers, one of which was bought by King Alfonso XIII of Spain. Varlet then designed marine engines to such purpose that Delahaye set up a new World's speed record for water of 54.50 km/h. Delahaye won, in fact, all the races for motor boats. The crowds of spectators were enormous, but the clients rare, so the nautical period ended and Delahaye began to make trucks, postal vans, break-down lorries, street-sweepers and fire engines. During the First World War, they made howitzers and armoured cars

1937

DELAHAYE 135MS

Figoni et Falaschi

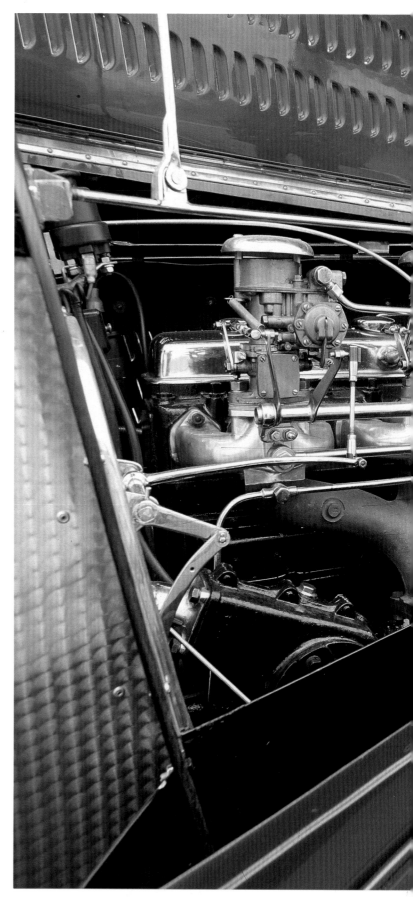

as well. But, more to the point, they had an opportunity, like many others, of self-education, making Marc Birkigt's V8 aero-engine. War over, they made tractors and an ingenious agricultural machine which ploughed several furrows simultaneously by machinery. At all times Delahaye's advertising pointed out that all these vehicles were modern. They even boasted that they were making everything by 'American' methods, by 1927, which was not strictly true, they were actually making cars which were dependable, robust, but in no way outstanding or distinguished. Honest, rugged and plain, they had a reputation for not breaking down. Prince Sixte de Bourbon, for example, in his 1929 mission to cross the Sahara in several directions, must have been pleased with the reliability of his Delahaye Type 104 'demi-camionnette'; well designed, rugged, and with no problems with either the car or the Sahara.

In 1934, however, Delahaye entered an entirely new era. The longevity of the engines and solidity of manufacture remained, but several new qualities appeared; style, speed, and individuality. This new dynamic Delahaye began to compete in motor sport and won several international records. Jean Françoise was the chief engineer who designed these new cars, starting with the 134, which became

with modifications that phenomenon, the 135. Delahaye used the 135 engine, with various modifications, for everything: the Alpine Cup, Monte Carlo Rally, Le Mans, and the Paris-Nice. Constructed for 20 years, that same engine, derated, was also used in fire engines, ambulances, armoured cars and trucks, as was the practice in the old days, but now with a better power unit altogether.

The 135 engine was a six-cylinder of 3227 cc or 3557 cc capacity, with a well designed camshaft and valve system and usually three carburettors, with a maximum of 4,300 rpm for competitions and 4,000 for normal vehicles, developing 90 to 155 bhp according to modifications and tune. It was capable, apparently, of anything. The later models, the 135M and MS, had an oil-cooler, as did the 148 which was simply a 135 with hydraulic dampers and different brakes. The chassis was underslung from 1935. There was independent front suspension, with a transverse spring and flat semi-elliptic at the rear, and Rudge wheels. The brakes, although cable operated, were of large diameter. The gearbox always had four speeds. The Wilson, or Cotal box which was available from 1937, more or less took over from the manual box.

The success of Jean François' 135 started in 1934. The 3,227 cc engine fitted in a short chassis monoposto won four world's records and eleven internationals at Montlhéry. Sadly, this actual car has disappeared.

In 1935, a 135 was fifth at Le Mans. 1936 brought sweeping success with eight wins including the GP de L'ACF at Montlhéry, Spa 24 hours and the Marseille GP in which Delahaye took the first six places! A chance to win at Le Mans, too, was denied them because the race was cancelled due to strikes. Nineteen thirty-seven saw five victories, amongst which the Donington 12 hours and the Monte Carlo Rally exemplify the cars' stamina, and a host of placings.

The 135 in fact had blown away the old saying *solide comme un Delahaye* and replaced it with an earned respect for a remarkably efficient piece of engineering, and fast.

The French coachbuilders, without exception, dressed the 135 with refined works of craftsmanship and art for twenty years, but in particular Chapron, Figoni et Falaschi, Letourneur et Marchand.

Delahaye took over Delage in 1935. They continued to make true Delage cars at first, later

Overleaf: DELAHAYE 135M, 1938, Figoni et Falaschi.

changing the engines to Delahaye. These cars actually achieved more success than the Delages had done in Concours d'Elégances, and in fact looked better even than the true Delages. There is a little edge between Delage and Delahaye owners at Delage/Delahaye Rallies. Delage feel that they have more art, refinement and style, and after all Delages *also* won the championship of the world in Grand Prix in 1927. Delahaye are *certain* that they have the most dependable engine in the world, and quite enough style. They are both right.

In 1938, the Type 145, a V12, achieved new records at the Montlhéry Circuit, and there was a Type 165, which was simply the street version of the 145. No one can state with certainty how many of these were actually made and sold. According to M. Moneing, head of the Bureau of Research at Delahaye, the materials necessary to make twelve were in the factory, but only four or five were actually completed. One was used on the turntable at the Delahaye stand at the 1938 Paris Saloon. There is a very grey area here, because it is known that 145 type chassis, originally designed for racing, have been transformed into roadsters, drophead coupés, sedancas and saloons, with coachwork which has 'walked' from less expensive and much less

DELAHAYE 135MS

De Villars

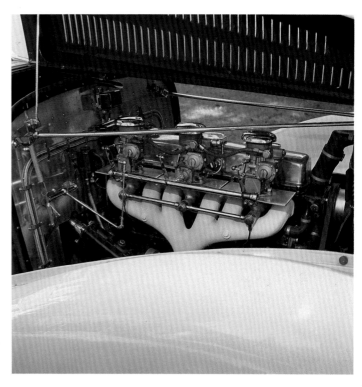

distinguished marques. As with Bentley but in reverse, where saloons are rebodied with Vanden Plas tourers in British racing green.

    Those who have carried out research with the coachbuilders have some acid remarks to make about (a) their deplorable lack of keeping accurate records as to which chassis received what coachwork,

DELAHAYE 135MS

Figoni et Falaschi

(b) regrettable imprecision about the dates of production, designs and final execution, and (c) their refusal to give precise answers to any questions, especially when asked at what date and for whom was a coachbuilt body draped over an old short chassis racing car?

Finally, how many Delahaye chassis for sport and prestige were constructed? An accurate answer is not possible because of war damage to records, but it is estimated that from 1934 to 1954 Delahaye produced 5,000 vehicles, of which 3,500 were made before the war. This would include Delahaye Types 134, 135, 145 and 148, together with the Delages.

There is always an interest in the number of cars which have survived. How many Delahayes? In 1975 there was a count of 200 in the world, of which 90 per cent were 135s.

As for the Delahaye 235, 83 were made and 50 to 60 have survived. Remarkable.

When the type 135 ceased to be made, because it finally really was old fashioned, Delahaye was taken over in 1954 by Hotchkiss and then they both disappeared soon afterwards, despite coming down to earth and making nothing but trucks.

9

TALBOT-LAGO

& Anthony Lago

Anthony Lago had most of the qualities which are needed to produce supercars: originality, engineering knowledge, administrative capacity and verve. While Birkigt lived at a period when he had to be a prime mover in all things, Lago could select, and he chose well, by borrowing the Bugatti concept of using the same power unit with variations, for GP, sports and Routières. His entire work is also nearer to the concepts of the eighties. It is therefore surprising and sad that there are so few Talbot-Lagos about. Precursors and forerunners as they were, they should have been fostered more.

Born in Venice in 1893, Anthony Lago received his training as an engineer at Milan Polytechnic. During the First World War, he was a Major in the Italian Army. In the 1920s he worked for Isotta-Fraschini; a good start. He came to England in the late twenties as their sales representative, but left to become technical director of L.A.P. Engineering. His next position was with the Wilson Self-Changing Gear Co. Ltd, where he finally became director general. This epicyclic gearbox had been designed by Major W.G. Wilson. During 1931 and 1932, Lago worked to such effect that Alvis, Crossley, Daimler, Invicta, Lanchester,

MG, Standard and Talbot were all using Wilson gearboxes as alternatives to manual boxes. Armstrong-Siddeley had used the Wilson box since 1929, because Lago used to drive for them in competition and he naturally persuaded them then. He also returned to Isotta-Fraschini and persuaded *them* to use the Wilson Pre-selector gearbox as well.

In 1933, Lago became a director of STD (Sunbeam-Talbot-Darracq). At this time, Owen Clegg, the English director-general of the Company, was considering that the French factory at Suresnes should be liquidated. It was too large and too complicated. Anthony Lago intervened and argued that the French part of the firm could be saved by a reorganisation. Lago was made director-general of the French part of STD, at Suresnes. The next year, the English half of STD was acquired by the Rootes group. Lago, who had now obtained considerable financial support, became the head of French Talbot. The year was 1934, and Anthony Lago was 41. He decided, like Bugatti and Coatalen, that participation in motor sport was an essential element, not for publicity alone, but actually for engineering integrity.

Just as Bugatti had produced cars for competition and then identical models in the sale room, so did Lago likewise. He had, in fact, three objectives when he started: (a) to make economies throughout the firm; (b) to change the Talbot concept towards lighter cars with a sporting image; and (c) to make the name Talbot-Lago mean something on the race tracks.

This was a radical change from the good but heavy Talbot image, created over the years by Owen Clegg. Lago's first step was to place the control of new research in the hands of Walter Becchia, the deputy head of engineering. The chief engineer, Vincenzo Bertarione, had been in charge since 1923 and was entrenched in his ways. Bertarione left soon after this to become chief engineer at Hotchkiss, where he remained, producing successful cars.

Walter Becchia, like Bertarione, had been trained at Fiat by Carlo Cavalli, when there were several brilliant engineers at work there including Bazzi, Cappa, Massimino and Zerbi. Working with Anthony Lago, Becchia was responsible for the successful Talbot-Lago engines. Throughout history there are invariably brilliant 'Man Fridays' close to the figurehead.

Lago made several other improvements, regrouping the services at 33 Quai du Général Gallieni, including a showroom for new cars. He also started a restaurant within the firm, where Lago himself dined with the workers and customers; an idea much vaunted at present because it is a custom of the Japanese so to harmonise management and workers, but this was 1934, forestalling by two years the trades-union cataclysms in France, and by fifty years the 'happy family' of management and workers all eating together *à la japonaise*.

Lago then turned his attention to the cars which had already been designed most recently by Bertarione and Becchia, to discover that their suspension system was simple, classical and first rate. So it was used on most models until 1945. A new six-cylinder engine, the T120, of 2,996 cc, was designed with hemispherical combustion chambers and overhead valves - it was the main element of the new Talbot. It produced 110 cv at 4000 rpm, with one Zenith carburettor and a compression ratio of 6.5 to 1. It was used in several models until 1939, in particular the Baby Sport, an excellent sports car, at a competitive price. 'Baby' just means small. Capital was still scarce, so the new model T150 actually had a T120 engine when it was shown at the 1935 salon. The period 1935/6/7 was difficult financially, partly because of the strikes, but Lago still brought out several new models, including the Baby, Major and Master at 3 litres, and the same models with 4-litre engines. The factory coachwork itself was well designed, but several French coachbuilders, including in particular Figoni et Falaschi, who were his friends, designed several versions of the famous 'Goutte d'eau' on the Baby chassis in 1938, and made really outstanding cars.

In fact Anthony Lago, in four years, had created a marque of some consequence.

In 1935 it was decided that the Grand Prix de l'ACF should be open to sports cars. The T12 of 3 litres was enlarged to 4 litres and named the T150C, (C for 'Course'), otherwise known as the Lago Special. The crankshaft was given seven bearings instead of four, and capacity was increased to 3,996 cc, bore and stroke being 90 x 104.5 mm. The liners were of nitrided steel with chrome at the base.

The aluminium pistons had three rings. The nitrided steel crankshaft was supported on bearings of phosphor bronze. The single camshaft was driven by pushrods. Lago hemispherical combustion chambers were peculiar to Anthony Lago and

TALBOT-LAGO T150SS

Figoni et Falaschi

considered to be an original development beyond other hemi-heads.

Fritz Fiedler's pushrod ohc engine, the 328 made for BMW in 1936, owed something to the Lago T150C, and consequently so, too, did Frazer Nash and Bristol as well, as they used the Fiedler engine.

In 1937, Lago engaged Lucien Girard of Zenith-Stromberg, to be part of the staff for competition, and he obtained 155 bhp at 4,500 rpm with a compression ratio of 7.4 to 1 for the Lago Special. Customers however, could only have 140 bhp at 4,100 rpm.

The Lago SS short chassis sports car weighed 130 kg less than the Lago Special and was capable of 160-180 km/h in normal form, and 200 km/h in competition. The Goutte d'eau was capable of 183.6 km/h and a Lago SS was third at Le Mans in 1938. From 1935 to 1937, Andreau, the chief designer of Figoni et Falaschi, created some of the most beautiful works of art on Lago chassis, culminating in a *Special Goutte d'Eau* for Duke Philippe de Massa (Chassis 90 117).

In 1936 the Talbot-Lagos did not win a single race. They simply could not match the pedigree or the performance of the Bugattis. Nineteen thirty-seven was a better year. They won the Tunis GP and the Miramas 3 hours, and a resounding 1-2-3 in the French GP itself. There was a third at Le Mans in 1938, Delahayes being first and second, but the real grim truth of that was that they were

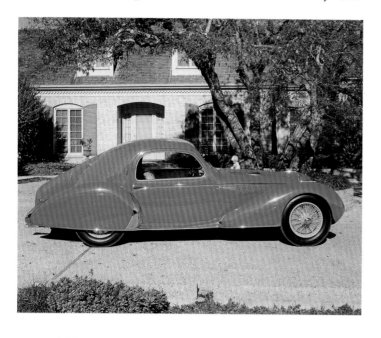

TALBOT-LAGO T150SS

Figoni et Falaschi

actually twelve laps behind the Sommer/Biondetti Alfa Romeo, until it broke a valve on Sunday afternoon.

At the Pau Grand Prix in 1939, Etancelin was third in a Talbot-Lago 4.5-litre, behind the Mercedes of Lang (first) and von Brauchitsch (second). Delahaye came 5-6-7-8, with 135s. The Talbot-Lago was two laps behind the Mercedes, and the Delahayes 8, 9, 12 and 14 laps behind. This put Jean François of Delahaye in his right place: remarkable but not so fabulous.

War ended sports car production at Suresnes for seven years, but it did not stop Anthony Lago thinking and working with his new engineer, Carlo Marchetti. They were both Italians, to whom the Second World War took second place to racing cars and a new engine which would win. From 1942 they were designing the 4.5-litre engine 2AC, using the pre-war chassis. Early in 1948 a new Grand Prix racing car was built with twin camshafts, operating inclined overhead valves through short pushrods. Reliable and with moderate fuel consumption, these cars won several major races during the next four seasons. Lago then converted this monoposto into a two-seater and Louis Rosier won the 1950 Le Mans in it, with another Talbot-Lago in second place. Le Mans had sixty entrants, the maximum number of starters in 1950, consisting of 26 different makes, with the French contingent the largest numerically, totalling 33. The winning Talbot-Lago set new records for average speed (89.7 mph) and distance (2,153 miles). Louis Rosier also set a new lap record at 102.83 mph.

The Lago Record of 1946, which had been designed during the war by Lago and Carlo Marchetti, put Talbot-Lago ahead for a while. There were 400 detail drawings in all. The capacity of 4.5 litres was to comply with the Formula 1 specifications for 1947-51, of 4.5 litres normally aspirated or 1.5 litres supercharged. Materials for manufacturing were in short supply, and the Régie Renault gained precedence because their cars were smaller and more popular, but Lago obtained sufficient steel to produce 125 Lago Record tourers. It is interesting that, due to the long period of gestation, this car was not subsequently modified, from 1946-55. There were of course considerable differences between the standard engines and the 'Grand Sport and Course'. This engine was named Lago 2AC. Lago admitted that while in England he had been impressed by Riley engines and also

TALBOT-LAGO T38 MAJOR

Talbot-Lago

by ERA which were based on them, and the 2AC is sure enough very similar, but with more attention to, and use of, the new metallurgy. The seven-bearing crankshaft was of mangano-siliceaux steel, for example. The two Zenith carburettors were fed by a mechanical fuel pump. The engine gave 170 bhp at 4,200 rpm with a compression ratio of 7 to 1 and a speed of 170 km/h was easily possible, despite the weight of the *carrosserie*.

Although the Lago Record was regarded as one of the best of the French post-war tourers, only 125 were sold in 1946, 160 in 1947 and 195 in 1948: 480 in all; insufficient to provide finances for the competition department. The 4½-litre Lago Record was *de rigueur* for all French politicians and directors, diplomats and personalities from 1946 to 50. One in particular, with the number plate 1 H75 and with coachwork by Saoutchik, was used by two successive Presidents, Vincent Auriol and René Coty. This was obviously not enough to save the firm.

It was therefore necessary to produce a smaller best seller, so a four-cylinder Lago Baby of 2.7-litres was presented at the Salon. This was really half of the Lago Record engine and the coachwork was too heavy for it. A six-cylinder version of the Record was made, but only a few dozen, as the financial situation was now desperate. The Rudge wheels were abandoned and even the Wilson

TALBOT-LAGO 150C

Figoni et Falaschi

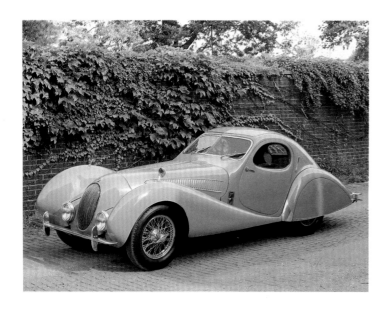

pre-selector(!) in favour of a normal manual box, being less expensive and absorbing less power. These various Baby Models were given 'pontoon' coachwork. By 1955 the Baby was withdrawn from the catalogue due to poor sales figures.

Between 1954 and 1955 a new tubular chassis was conceived for the Lago 2500 which would be suitable for sports and competition cars. The chassis, revised suspension and road holding were all splendid, but the engine was not so good as the old 4.5-litre (nor that of the Ferrari 250 Europa or even the Lancia Aurelia). Sadly, only fifteen of the new Coupé Lago 2500s were sold. Realising

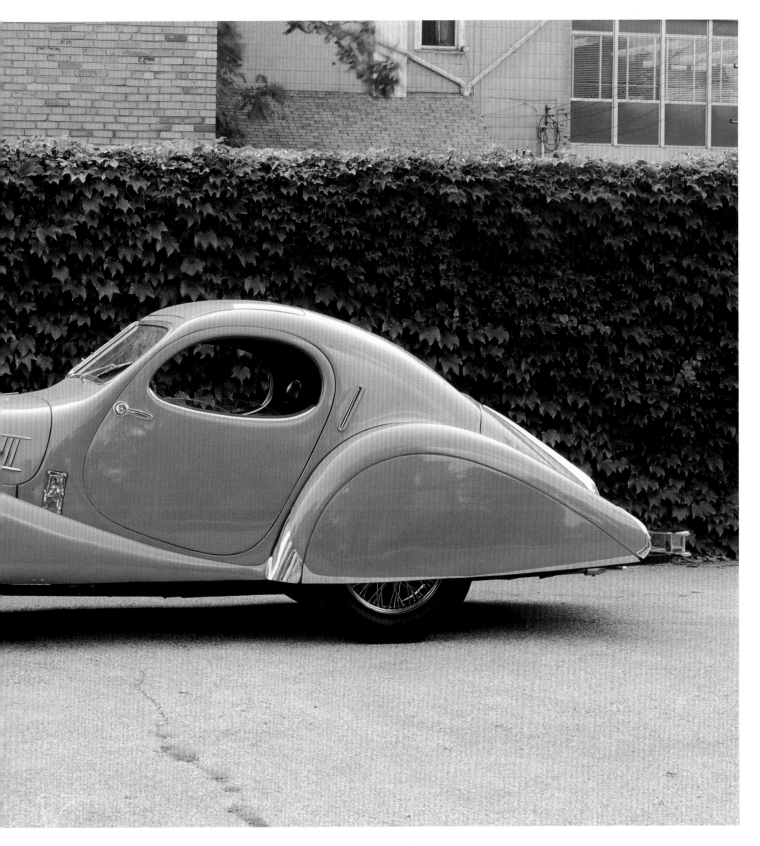

TALBOT-LAGO RECORD

Talbot-Lago

that it was the fault of the engine, and now desperate, Lago turned to BMW. They provided, at his request, their V8 with the bore reduced to 72.5 from 74 mm, producing a capacity of 2,476 cc. The BMW gave 138 bhp and it had a ZF gearbox. This hybrid was baptised 'Lago America'. *Road and Track* magazine gave it a good review and were pleased at its 190 km/h, but, even so, only 12 cars were sold in the USA, this being the total production.

TALBOT-LAGO 2500 SPORT

Franay

Simca took over Talbot-Lago in 1959 and fitted their Simca V8 engine to the remaining handful of chassis. A sad end.

Fate and the Receiver can be unjust. Lago actually had drive and prescience. The Lago SS, Grand Sport and Record in particular, were ahead of their time in both engineering and coachwork, as the Baby and Lago Special had been pre-war. Talbot-Lagos had a brilliant record in competition despite being hampered by lack of funds and occasional bad luck. Anthony Lago's integrity and intensity, engineering expertise and feeling for style are evident in everything he made. Defeated by accountancy and the financial climate of France in the late fifties his cars continued to win respect. They are much nearer to the cars of the eighties than Delage and Hispano, which are fabulous and gloriously of the thirties, whereas the Talbot-Lagos were ahead of their time. Many ask how Anthony Lago took the failure of his company in 1959, after years of continuously intense effort and quite remarkable success in competition: he died in 1960.

168

TECHNICAL SPECIFICATIONS

Marque	Hispano-Suiza
Type	Alfonso
Date Built	1911-1914
Engine	Straight 4
Bore & Stroke	80x180 mm
Capacity	3620 cc
Power output	57 bhp @ 2,300 rpm
Carburettor	Single Hispano
Gearbox	3-speed
	4-speed after 1912
Clutch	Multiplate, cone after 1912
Suspension	Semi-elliptic F & R, $\frac{3}{4}$-elliptic R after 1912
Brakes	Transmission brake and internal expanding rear brakes
Wheelbase	8 ft 8 in (2.65 m) or 9 ft 10 in (2.73 m) from 1912
Track	4 ft 1 in (1.23 m) rear track 4 ft 3 in (1.24 m) on long wheelbase
Length	—
Weight	1460 lb (657 kg) short, 1680 lb (756 kg) long wheelbase
Bhp/litre	15.745
Fuel con.	20 mpg

Marque	Hispano-Suiza
Type	H6B (H6C, 1924)
Date Built	1919-1938
Engine	In-line 6
Bore & stroke	100x140 mm
Capacity	6597 cc
Power output	135 bhp @ 3000 rpm (H6C, 200 bhp)
Carburettor	Single updraught Hispano-Suiza
Gearbox	3-speed manual/synchro in unit with engine
Clutch	Multiplate, dry
Suspension	Semi-elliptic springs F & R
Brakes	Servo assisted 4WB
Wheelbase	12 ft 1 in (368 cm)
Track	4 ft 8 in (142 cm)
Length	15 ft 10 in (482.6 cm)
Weight	3.360 lb (1.524 kg)
Bhp/litre	20.463 (H6C, 25)
Fuel con.	15 mpg

Marque	Hispano-Suiza
Type	Type 68 J12
Date Built	1931-1938
Engine	V12 60°
Bore & stroke	100x100 mm
Capacity	9424 cc
Power output	220 bhp @ 3000 rpm (6:1 CR), 180 bhp @ 3000 rpm (5:1 CR)
Carburettor	2 downdraught twin-choke Hispano-Suiza
Gearbox	3-speed manual, no synchro at first 1931-1934 right-hand levers and twin magnetos 1935-1938 central gear lever
Clutch	Multiplate, dry
Suspension	Semi-elliptic F & R: offset front, shorter than rear
Brakes	4 wheel servo-assisted drum
Wheelbase	11 ft 3 in (3.43 m); 12 ft 2 in (3.70 m); 12' 6" (3.80 m) or 13 ft 2 in (4.01 m)
Track	4 ft 9 in (1.2 m), but 4 ft 11 in (1.5 m) with longest track
Length	16 ft (4.949 m)
Weight	4,900 lb (2,227 kg)
Bhp/litre	23.344
Fuel con.	10 mpg

Marque	Hispano-Suiza
Type	K6
Date Built	1933-1938
Engine	Straight 6
Bore & stroke	100x110 mm
Capacity	5184 cc
Power output	Not stated
Carburettor	Downdraught H.S
Gearbox	3-speed manual: central gear lever
Clutch	Single, dry plate
Suspension	Semi-elliptic F & R
Brakes	4-wheel servo-assisted drum
Wheelbase	11 ft 3 in (3.43 m) or 12 ft 2½ in (3.72 m)
Track	4 ft 9 in (1.44 m)
Length	15 ft 2 in (4.62 m)
Weight	35 cwt
Bhp/litre	—
Fuel con.	14-17 mpg

Marque	Bugatti
Type	Type 41
Date Built	1927-1933
Engine	Straight 8
Bore & stroke	125x130 mm
Capacity	12763 cc
Power output	300 bhp @ 2000 rpm
Carburettor	Single updraught Bugatti
Gearbox	3-speed manual gearbox mounted in unit, with straight bevel
Clutch	Multi-plate running in oil
Suspension	F; ½-elliptic leaf R; 2 sets of ¼-elliptic leaf springs, 1 for normal, together for heavy loads
Brakes	Cable without servo assistance
Wheelbase	14 ft 2 in (4.26 m)
Track	5 ft 3 in (1.59 m)
Length	22 ft (6.6 m)
Weight	5600 lb (2540 kg)
Bhp/litre	23.5
Fuel con.	Not stated

Marque	Bugatti
Type	Type 44
Date Built	1927
Engine	Straight 8
Bore & stroke	69x100 mm
Capacity	2992 cc
Power output	Not stated
Carburettor	Schebler
Gearbox	4-speed, separate from engine
Clutch	Multi-plate in oil
Suspension	F; semi-elliptics R; ¼-elliptics/Bugatti system/reversed
Brakes	Cable/aluminium drums
Wheelbase	10 ft 3 in (3.12 m)
Track	4 ft 0 in (1.23 m)
Length	—
Weight	1980 lb (900 kg)
Bhp/litre	—
Fuel con.	25 mpg (at 85 mph)

Marque	Bugatti
Type	Type 46
Date Built	1929-1930
Engine	Straight 8
Bore & stroke	81x130 mm
Capacity	5227 cc
Power output	—
Carburettor	Multi jet Smith
Gearbox	3-speed, in unit with rear axle: central lever. Rubber mounted fly wheel with hub & rubber ring
Clutch	Multi disc with Ferodo facings, dry
Suspension	F; half elliptics R; Reversed $\frac{1}{4}$-elliptic springs/Bugatti system
Brakes	Aluminium brake drums of 15.75 inch diameter/servo
Wheelbase	11 ft 2 in (3.50 m)
Track	4 ft 6 in (140 m)
Length	13 ft 1 in (3.9 m)
Weight	2530 lb (1150 kg)
Bhp/litre	—
Fuel con.	15 mpg

Marque	Bugatti
Type	Type 49
Date Built	1930-1934
Engine	Straight 8
Bore & stroke	72x100 mm
Capacity	3257 cc
Power output	—
Carburettor	Single updraught, Schebler
Gearbox	4-speed manual: central lever, direct
Clutch	Dry plate
Suspension	F; by $\frac{1}{2}$-elliptic leaf springs R; Reversed cantilever $\frac{1}{4}$-elliptics & torque rod from axle to frame
Brakes	—
Wheelbase	10 ft 7 in (3.23 m)
Track	4 ft 2 in (1.27 m)
Length	13 ft 9 in (4.19 m)
Weight	2150 lb (975 kg)
Bhp/litre	—
Fuel con.	25 mpg

Marque	Bugatti
Type	Type 50 (Type 50T)
Date Built	1930
Engine	Straight 8
Bore & stroke	86x107 mm
Capacity	4972 cc
Power output	200 bhp @ 4000 rpm
Carburettor	2 Schebler mounted below supercharger
Gearbox	Central lever/gearbox at back axle
Clutch	Dry disc
Suspension	F; $\frac{1}{2}$-elliptics R; Reversed $\frac{1}{4}$-elliptic springs/Bugatti
Brakes	Servo-assisted
Wheelbase	9 ft 8 in (3.10 m)
Track	4 ft 6 in (1.40 m)
Length	13 ft (3.983 m)
Weight	2530 lb (1150 kg)
Bhp/litre	40.225
Fuel con.	—

Marque	Bugatti
Type	Type 57
Date Built	1934-1936 (original model)
Power output	140 bhp @ 4,990 rpm

Type	Type 57S
Date Built	1935
	Higher CR 8:5:1
	Dry sump
	Double plate clutch
	Dash mounted Scintilla Vertex magnets
	De Ram shock absorbers
	Lower chassis with rear axle passing through frame
	V radiator
	Front axle in halves

Type	Type 57: Series 2
Date Built	1936-7
	Rubber mounted engine
	More cross bracing to chassis
	More instruments to dash board
	Modified exhaust magnified

Type	Type 57C
Date Built	1937/8
	Supercharger fitted to standard model

Type	Type 57 SC
	Supercharger fitted to the 57S 125 mph
	Both 57S and 57SC withdrawn after 1938, as too expensive to manufacture

Type	Type 57: Series 3
	Hydraulic brakes Bugatti-Lockhead type
	De Ram shock absorbers replaced by telescopic Alliquant

Marque	Bugatti
Type	Type 57S (57C, 57S, SC)
Date Built	1936-39
Engine	Straight 8
Bore & stroke	72x100 mm
Capacity	3257 cc
Power output	175 bhp @ 5,500 rpm
Carburettor	Single updraught Zenith
Gearbox	4-speed manual without synchromesh, central lever
Clutch	Twin dry plate
Suspension	F; semi elliptic leaf R; reversed cantilever $\frac{1}{4}$-elliptics and torque rod from axle to frame
Brakes	Rod and cable brakes/hydraulic assisted
Wheelbase	9 ft 9 in (2.9 m)
Track	4 ft 5 in (1.35 m)
Length	13 ft 3 in (3.97 m)
Weight	2100 lb (952 kg)
Bhp/litre	53.73
Fuel con.	—

Marque	Delage
Type	D8 & D8S (Sport)
Date Built	1929-1935
Engine	Straight 8
Bore & stroke	77x109 mm
Capacity	4,050 cc
Power output	120 bhp @ 4000 rpm (D85, 118 bhp @ 3800 rpm)
Carburettor	Smith-Barraquand 5-jet
Gearbox	4-speed manual (without synchromesh) in unit with engine; central gearlever
Clutch	Single dry plate
Suspension	$\frac{1}{2}$-elliptic leaf springs F and R and torque rods
Brakes	Shaft and cable operated drum brakes, hand brake on all wheels. Clayton Dewandre servo and Dewandre-Repusseau
Wheelbase	10 ft 10 in (3.32 m), (D8S, 11 ft 11 in, 3.75 m)
Track	4 ft 8 in (1.41 m)
Length	16 ft (4.8 m)
Weight	4,400 lb (1995 kg)
Bhp/litre	25.5 (D8S, 29.5)
Fuel con.	12 mpg

Marque	Delage
Type	D5, D6 & D6/65
Date Built	1931-1833 (D6/75, 1934-35)
Engine	Straight 6
Bore & stroke	77x109 mm (D6/75, 81x9.05 mm)
Capacity	3045 cm (D6/75, 2800 cc)
Power output	72 bhp @ 3600 rpm (D6/75, 72 bhp @ 4200 rpm)
Carburettor	Delage carburettor (Smith Barraquand licence)
Gearbox	4-speed gearbox, 2 with synchromesh, central gearlever
Clutch	Single, dry disc
Suspension	Semi elliptic F and R
Brakes	4-wheel drum brakes
Wheelbase	9 ft 9 in (3.114 m) & 10 ft 6 in (3.249 m)
Track	F; 4 ft 5 in (1.36 m) R; 4 ft 8 in (1.42 m)
Length	14 ft (4.28 m) & 14 ft 4 in (4.41 m)
Weight	2690 lb (1,200 kg)
Bhp/litre	24
Fuel con.	22 mpg

DELAGE/DELAHAYE

In 1937, the D6/60 was bored out to 77 from 74 mm and the bhp increased from 58 to 60.

The D6/65 became the D6/70 by boring out to 80 from 79.25 m, making the capacity 2729 cc. In both cases an optional Cotal gearbox was available. The D6/70 had a notable success, with bodies by Letourneur and Marchand. The D6/80 remained unchanged.

The D8/100 ceased production, and a new type the D8/120 was produced. The D8/120 was given a Delahaye engine of 4750 cc with a power output of 115 bhp @ 4,200 rpm and a lowered chassis.

Marque	Delage
Type	D6-11 & D11S (sport)
Date Built	1932-1934
Engine	Straight 6
Bore & stroke	75x75.5 mm
Capacity	2000 cm
Power output	68 @ 4,500 rpm
Carburettor	Smith-Barraquand, 5-jet
Gearbox	4-speed, 3rd and 4th synchromesh
Clutch	Single, dry plate
Suspension	F; independent by transverse spring R; semi-elliptic
Brakes	Cable: duo servo: hand brake on all four
Wheelbase	10 ft (3.06 m) normal & 10 ft 3 in (3.26 m) long wheelbase
Track	4 ft 8 in (1.45 m)
Length	—
Weight	2690 lb (1,200 kg)
Bhp/litre	34
Fuel con.	25 mpg

Marque	Delage
Type	D8/85 and D8/105
Date Built	1935
Engine	Straight 8 cylinders
Bore & stroke	79.25x90.5 mm 80x107 mm*
Capacity	4300 cc* 3570 cc
Power output	D8/85 85 bhp @ 4000 rpm (D8/105 102 bhp @ 3800 rpm) 90 bhp @ 3900 rpm*
Carburettor	Smith Barraquand
Gearbox	4-speed manual, 2 with synchromesh; central gearlever Cotal gearbox*
Clutch	Single, dry plate
Suspension	½-elliptic leaf springs F and R and torque rods
Brakes	Shaft and cable operated drum brakes, hand brake on all wheels. Clayton Dewandre servo and Dewandre-Repusseau
Wheelbase	10 ft 10 in (3.32 m)
Track	4 ft 8 in (1.41 m)
Length	16 ft (4.8 m)
Weight	2690 lb (1200 kg)
Bhp/litre	24
Fuel con.	22 mpg

*Items marked by an asterisk relate to the later model fitted with a Delahaye engine after abandonment of the Michelat unit

Marque	Delage/Delahaye
Type	Type D180
Date Built	1947
Engine	Delahaye 175/180
Bore & stroke	94x107 mm
Capacity	4455 cc
Power output	140 @ 4000 rpm
Carburettor	Solex 40 AIP or 3 Solex, giving 160 bhp
Gearbox	Cotal electromagnetic
Clutch	2 discs, dry
Suspension	System Dubonnet: independent front
Brakes	—
Wheelbase	10 ft 8 in (3.32 m)
Track	F; 4 ft 7 in (1.59 m)
Length	R; 4 ft 9 in (1.52 m)
Weight	4730 lb (2150 kg)
Bhp/litre	—
Fuel con.	18-22 mpg

Marque	Delahaye
Type	Type 148
Date Built	1935-1939
Engine	Straight 6
Bore & stroke	84x107 mm
Capacity	3557 cc
Power output	85 bhp
Carburettor	Inverted SNI
Gearbox	4-speed manual, or Cotal
Clutch	Single, dry disc
Suspension	F-independent R-by flat semi-elliptics
Brakes	Auto Serreurs
Wheelbase	10 ft 10 in (3.350 m)
Track	F; 4 ft 9 in (1.450 m)
	R; 4 ft 10 in (1.500 m)
Length	15 ft (4.580 m)
Weight	2310 lb (1050 kg)
Bhp/litre	23.89
Fuel con.	15 mpg

Marque	Delahaye
Type	Type 135
Date Built	1935-1950
Engine	Straight 6
Bore & stroke	80x107 mm (84x107 mm, competition)
Capacity	3237 cc (3557 cc, competition)
Power output	130 @ 3850 (160 @ 4200, competition)
Carburettor	3 downdraught Solex
Gearbox	4-speed synchromesh manual (not on 1st)
Clutch	Single, dry plate
Suspension	F; transverse leaf springs and wishbones
	R; ½-elliptic leaf
Brakes	4-wheel drum and Bendix servo
Wheelbase	9 ft 8 in (2.94 m)
Track	4 ft 7 in (1.41 m)
Length	15 ft (4.5 m)
Weight	2750 lb (1247 kg)
Bhp/litre	40.16 (1935) 45.0 (1950)
Fuel con.	22-25 mpg

Marque	Delahaye
Type	Type 175
Date Built	1945-1955
Engine	Straight 6
Bore & stroke	94x107 mm
Capacity	4500 cc
Power output	140 bhp
Carburettor	Inverted
Gearbox	Cotal
Clutch	2 disc, dry
Suspension	F; independent/Dubonet R; semi-elliptic
Brakes	Hydraulic
Wheelbase	9 ft 5 in (2.95 m)
Track	F; 4 ft 9 in (1.45 m) R; 5 ft (1.53 m)
Length	15 ft 1 in (4.62 m)
Weight	3010 lb (1050 kg)
Bhp/litre	31
Fuel con.	18 mpg

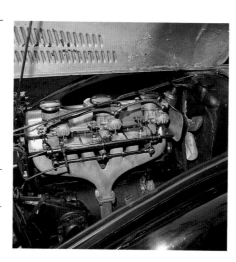

Marque	Delahaye
Type	Type 178
Date Built	1945-1955
Engine	Straight 6
Bore & stroke	94x107 mm
Capacity	4500 cc
Power output	140 bhp
Carburettor	Inverted
Gearbox	Cotal
Clutch	2-disc dry
Suspension	F; independent/Dubonet R; semi-elliptic
Brakes	Hydraulic
Wheelbase	10 ft 3 in (3.15 m)
Track	F; 4 ft 9 in (1.45 m) R; 5 ft (1.53 m)
Length	15 ft 8 in (4.82 m)
Weight	2343 lb (1065 kg)
Bhp/litre	31
Fuel con.	18 mpg

Marque	Delahaye
Type	Type 180
Date Built	1945-1955
Engine	Straight 6
Bore & stroke	94x107 mm
Capacity	4500 cc
Power output	140 bhp
Carburettor	Inverted
Gearbox	Cotal
Clutch	2-disc, dry
Suspension	F; independent/Dubonet R; semi-elliptic
Brakes	Hydraulic
Wheelbase	10 ft 9 in (3.33 m)
Track	F; 4 ft 9 in (1.45 m) R; 5 ft (1.53 m)
Length	16 ft 5 in (5.02 m)
Weight	2409 lb (1095 kg)
Bhp/litre	31
Fuel con.	18 mpg

Marque	Delahaye
Type	Type 235
Date Built	1952-1954
Engine	Straight 6
Bore & stroke	84x107 mm
Capacity	3557 cc
Power output	152 bhp @ 4,200 rpm
Carburettor	3 Solex
Gearbox	Cotal
Clutch	2 disc/dry
Suspension	Improved independent suspension F and R with cranked design
Brakes	Hydraulic
Wheelbase	9 ft 7 in (2.95 m)
Track	F; 4 ft 7 in (1.40 m) R; 4 ft 10 in (1.48 m)
Length	16 ft 6 in (5.10 m)
Weight	3256 lb (1480 kg)
Bhp/litre	42.73
Fuel con.	20 mpg

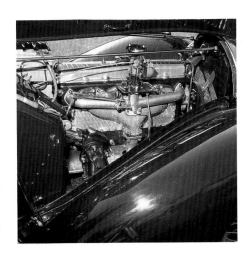

Marque	Talbot-Lago
Type	T15
Date Built	1936-1939
Engine	Straight 6
Bore & stroke	74x104.5 mm
Capacity	2696 cc
Power output	75 bhp
Carburettor	Zenith-Stromberg
Gearbox	4-speed manual, or Wilson Preselector
Clutch	Single, dry disc
Suspension	F; independent R; semi-elliptic
Brakes	—
Wheelbase	Baby; 9 ft 4 in (2.95 m) Cadette; 10 ft 5 in (3.20 m)
Track	Baby; F 4 ft 6 in (1.38 m) R 4 ft 8 in (1.46 m) Cadette; F 4 ft 6 in (1.38 m) R 4 ft 8 in (1.46 m)
Length	Baby; 16 ft (2.90 m) Cadette; 17 ft (5.20 m)
Weight	Baby; 3190 lb (1450 kg) Cadette; 3278 lb (1490 kg)
Bhp/litre	27.88
Fuel con.	18-20 mpg

Marque	Talbot-Lago
Type	Minor T4
Date Built	1937-1939
Engine	Straight 6
Bore & stroke	86x100 mm
Capacity	2.323 cc
Power output	62 bhp @ 4000 rpm
Carburettor	Stromberg
Gearbox	4-speed, Wilson preselector
Clutch	Single, dry disc
Suspension	F; independent R; semi-elliptic
Brakes	4-wheel brakes/cable and Bendix
Wheelbase	9 ft 4 in (2.95 m)
Track	F; 4 ft 6 in (1.38 m) R; 4 ft 8 in (1.46 m)
Length	15 ft 8 in (4.80 m)
Weight	2970 lb (1350 kg)
Bhp/litre	26.689
Fuel con.	24 mpg

Marque	Talbot-Lago
Type	T120
	3 litre
	Major 5 seats
Date Built	1937-1939
Engine	Straight 6
Bore &	
stroke	78x104.5 mm
Capacity	2.996 cc
Power output	90 bhp @
	4000 rpm
Carburettor	Zenith-Stromberg
Gearbox	4-speed synchromesh
	or Wilson
	preselector
Clutch	Single, dry disc
Suspension	F; independent
	R; semi-elliptic
Brakes	Cable, Bendix
Wheelbase	10 ft 4 in (3.20 m)
Track	F; 4 ft 2 in
	(1.28 m)
	R; 4 ft 9 in
	(1.46 m)
Length	16 ft 10 in (5.20 m)
Weight	3322 lb (1510 kg)
Bhp/litre	30
Fuel con.	24 mpg

Marque	Talbot-Lago
Type	T17
	3 litre
	Baby 4 seats
Date Built	1937-1939
Engine	Straight 6
Bore &	
stroke	78x104.5 mm
Capacity	2.996 cc
Power output	90 bhp @
	4000 rpm
Carburettor	Zenith-Stromberg
Gearbox	4-speed synchromesh
	or Wilson
	preselector
Clutch	Single, dry disc
Suspension	F; independent
	R; semi-elliptic
Brakes	Cable, Bendix, 12
	inch drums
Wheelbase	9 ft 4 in (2.95 m)
Track	F; 4 ft 6 in
	(1.38 m)
	R; 4 ft 9 in
	(1.46 m)
Length	15 ft 11 in (4.90 m)
Weight	3322 lb (1500 kg)
Bhp/litre	30
Fuel con.	24 mpg

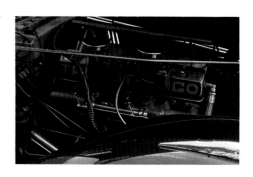

Marque	Talbot-Lago
Type	T150 (Lago Special)
Date Built	1938-1939
Engine	Straight 6
Bore &	
stroke	90x104.5 mm
Capacity	3996 cc
Power output	140 bhp @
	4000 rpm
Carburettor	3 Strombergs
Gearbox	4-speed, synchro
	manual or Wilson
	preselector
Clutch	dry
Suspension	F; independent
	R; semi-elliptic
Brakes	Cable, Bendix, 14
	inch drums
Wheelbase	9 ft 6 in (2.95 m)
Track	F; 4 ft 6 in
	(1.38 m)
	R; 4 ft 8 in
	(1.46 m)
Length	16 ft (4.90 m)
Weight	3278 lb (1490 kg)
Bhp/litre	35.03
Fuel con.	20-22 mpg

Marque	Talbot-Lago
Type	T150C (Lago SS)
Date Built	1938-1939
Engine	Straight 6
Bore & stroke	90x104.5 mm
Capacity	3.996 litres
Power output	140 bhp @ 4000 rpm
Carburettor	3 Strombergs
Gearbox	4-speed, synchro manual or Wilson preselector
Clutch	dry
Suspension	F, independent R; semi-elliptic
Brakes	Cable, Bendix, 14 inch drums
Wheelbase	8 ft 5 in (2.65 m)
Track	F; 4 ft 5 in (1.32 m) R; 4 ft 4 in (1.32 m)
Length	14 ft 5 in (4.37 m)
Weight	2640 lb (1200 kg)
Bhp/litre	35.03
Fuel con.	20-22 mpg

Marque	Talbot-Lago
Type	4-litre Baby 4 seats
Date Built	1938-1939
Engine	Straight 6
Bore & stroke	90x104.5 mm
Capacity	3996 cc
Power output	91 bhp @ 4000 rpm
Carburettor	Zenith-Stromberg
Gearbox	Wilson preselector
Clutch	dry
Suspension	F; independent R; semi-elliptic
Brakes	Cable, Bendix, 14 inch drums
Wheelbase	9 ft 6 in (2.95 m)
Track	F; 4 ft 6 in (1.38 m) R; 4 ft 7 in (1.46 m)
Length	16 ft (4.9 m)
Weight	3278 lb (1490 kg)
Bhp/litre	22.77
Fuel con.	18-20 mpg

Marque	Talbot-Lago
Type	4-litre Major 5 seats
Date Built	1938-1939
Engine	Straight 6
Bore & stroke	90x104.5 mm
Capacity	3996 cc
Power output	91 bhp @ 4000 rpm
Carburettor	Zenith-Stromberg
Gearbox	Wilson preselector
Clutch	dry
Suspension	F; independent R; semi-elliptic
Brakes	Cable, Bendix, 14 inch drums
Wheelbase	10 ft 5 in (3.2 m)
Track	F; 4 ft 6 in (1.38 m) R; 4 ft 7 in (1.46 m)
Length	17 ft (5.2 m)
Weight	3366 lb (1530 kg)
Bhp/litre	22.77
Fuel con.	18-20 mpg

Marque	Talbot-Lago
Type	4-litre Master 7 seats
Date Built	1938-1939
Engine	Straight 6
Bore & stroke	90x104.5 mm
Capacity	3996 cc
Power output	91 bhp @ 4000 rpm
Carburettor	Zenith-Stromberg
Gearbox	—
Clutch	—
Suspension	F; independent R; semi-elliptic
Brakes	Cable, Bendix, 14 inch drums
Wheelbase	11 ft 3 in (3.45 m)
Track	F; 4 ft 6 in (1.38 m) R; 4 ft 7 in (1.46 m)
Length	17 ft 2 in (5.3 m)
Weight	3630 lb (1650 kg)
Bhp/litre	22.77
Fuel con.	18-20 mpg

PHOTO CREDITS

Photographs are shown by page number and postion under the photographer's or supplier's name.

Where known the name of the owner of the subject car is given in brackets following the page number.

David Sparrow
2/3 (Philippe Looten), 7 (José Lesur), 8, 11, 12 (Bernard Heurteux), 21 (José Lesur), 23, 31 (Jean-Paul Dubroca), 34 (Geoffrey Perfect), 36, 38, 50/51 (Bernard Heurteux), 52/3, 68-73 (Geoffrey Perfect), 76l (Geoffrey Perfect), 77-79 (Geoffrey Perfect), 80/81 (Geoffrey Perfect), 98-101 (Geoffrey Perfect), 106 (José Lesur), 113 (José Lesur), 118-120 (José Lesur), 132-135 (José Lesur), 138 (Roger Tanguy), 139, 146/147 (Roger Tanguy), 148/149 (Philippe Looten), 152 (Michel Potelle), 160/161 (Roger Tanguy), 164-167 (Michel Potelle), 168/169 (Roger Martin), 172t, 172c, 173, 175t, 176-181, 184.

Jerry McCabe
15 (Ray Middleton), 25 (Frank Annett), 27 (Bernard Parris), 38 (Ray Middleton), 40-43 (Bernard Parris), 46-49 (Adrian Liddell), 54-57 (Ray Middleton), 58-65 (Centre Historique de l'Auto, Reims), 82/83 (Brian Dearden-Briggs), 94/95 (Centre Historique de l'Auto), 109 (Frank Annett), 110/111 (W. Bayley), 114/115, 116 (Tom Bowhill), 122-125 (Frank Annett), 128-131 (Frank Annett), 150l/l (Centre Historique de l'Auto), 172r.

Len Smith
28 (Peter Agg), 69, 84/85 (John Wilson), 86 (H.R.G. Conway), 91 (Peter Agg), 92/93 (Ivan Dutton), 96/97 (John Merryfield), 102/103 (Midland Motor Museum), 104/105 (Peter Agg), 140-145 (Peter Agg), 174.

Max de Roche
12 (Bernard Heurteux), 16 (José Lesur), 76r (Ian Finlater), 112l (José Lesur) 175.

Sotheby's
32, 44/45, 66, 88, 127, 136, 150t, 151.

Automobile Quarterly
74, 156/157, 162/163.

Haymarket Publishing
75, 158.

Andrew Morland
170.

Christies
18.

P. Strinati
137.